We are BIGGER *than* RELIGION

THE CHURCH HAS BECOME TRANSCULTURAL, 'CATHO-PENTECOSTAL,' VISUAL AND MATERIAL CULTURE.

By Dr. Alan Pateman

BY DR. JENNIFER PATEMAN

AVAILABLE FROM **APMI** PUBLICATIONS,
AMAZON.COM AND OTHER RETAIL OUTLETS

We are BIGGER *than* RELIGION

DR. ALAN PATEMAN

Profitable Instruction

There's nothing like the written Word of God for showing you the way to salvation through faith in Christ Jesus. **Every part of Scripture is God-breathed and useful one way or another -** <u>showing us truth,</u> <u>exposing our rebellion,</u> <u>correcting our mistakes,</u> **<u>training us to live God's way</u>**. *Through the Word we are put together and shaped up for the tasks God has for us.*

(2 Timothy 3:16 MSG)

BOOK TITLE:
We are Bigger than Religion

WRITTEN BY Dr. ALAN PATEMAN
Paperback ISBN: 978-1-909132-23-8
Hardcover ISBN: 978-1-909132-25-2
eBook ISBN: 978-1-909132-24-5

Published By:
APMI Publications
In Partnership with Truth for the Journey Books **46**
Email: publications@alanpateman.com
www.AlanPatemanMinistries.com

Acknowledgements:
Author/Design/Senior Editor/Publisher: Apostle Dr. Alan Pateman
Editing/Proofreading/Research: Dr. Jennifer Pateman
Computer Administration/Office Manager: Dr. Dorothea Struhlik
Cover Image Credit: thecatholicsun.com, Creator: Paul Haring, Copyright: © 2016 Catholic News Service

Unless otherwise indicated, all scriptural quotations are from the HOLY BIBLE, NEW INTERNATIONAL VERSION ®. NIV ®. Copyright © 1973, 1978, 1984 by the International Bible Society. Used by permission of Zondervan Publishing House. All rights reserved.

*Where scriptures appear with special emphasis (**in bold,** italic or <u>underlined</u>) we have edited them ourselves in order to bring focused attention within the context of this subject being taught.*

❖

Dedication

This dedication is for all those who have ears to hear, and are not afraid of hearing the voice of God's Prophets. Satan has undermined the authority of the *"prophet and his voice"* in every generation, including this one – simply because they threaten him the most by revealing his deceptions!

Remember that God Himself singles them out when He declares, *"Come not against mine anointed ones, and against my prophets do no evil"* (1 Chronicles 16:22 YLT). They will always be "singled-out" so we must not be timid about them. Instead let us become a generation that develops "ears to hear" the voice of His Prophets – resisting our human instinct that "despises" this gift.

They may not be as "smooth-talking" as the other gifts *(even much less articulate perhaps)* especially to the humanistic crowd; but oh how we need this potent gift in the Body of Christ RIGHT NOW!

Amen

❖

Letters to the Church

❖

Acknowledgement

This book "We are BIGGER than RELIGION" is made up of 25 Truths for the Journey's that are Dr Alan's Letters to the Church, an apostolic and prophetic voice.

His heart is to equip believers with relevant teaching as God directs, that would cause them to be victorious and well established in their pursuit to detangle themselves from religion so they can follow their divine race.

❖

Poem

Why I Hate Religion, But Love Jesus
By Jefferson Bethke

What if I told you Jesus came to abolish religion?
I mean, if religion is so great, why has it started so many wars?
Why does it build huge churches but fails to feed the poor?
Tells single moms God doesn't love them if they've ever had a divorce
But in the Old Testament, God actually calls religious people whores

Religion might preach grace, but another thing they practice
Tend to ridicule God's people; they did it to John the Baptist
They can't fix their problems, and so they just mask it
Not realizing religion's like spraying perfume on a casket
See, the problem with religion is it never gets to the core
It's just behavior modification, like a long list of chores
Like, "Let's dress up the outside, make it look nice and neat"
But it's funny that's what they used to do to mummies
while the corpse rots underneath

Now I ain't judging; I'm just saying, quit putting on a fake look
'Cause there's a problem if people only know you're a Christian
by your Facebook
I mean, in every other aspect of life, you know that logic's unworthy
It's like saying you play for the Lakers just because you bought a jersey
See, this was me too, but no one seemed to be on to me
Acting like a church kid while addicted to pornography
See, on Sunday I'd go to church, but Saturday getting faded
Acting if I was simply created to just have sex and get wasted
See, I spent my whole life building this facade of neatness
But now that I know Jesus, I boast in my weakness

Because if grace is water, then the Church should be an ocean
It's not a museum for good people — it's a hospital for the broken
Which means I don't have to hide my failure;
I don't have to hide my sin
Because it doesn't depend on me; it depends on Him
See, because when I was God's enemy and certainly not a fan
He looked down and said, "I want that man."
Which is why Jesus hated religion, and for it He called them fools
Don't you see so much better than just following some rules
Now let me clarify — I love the Church, I love the Bible,
and yes, I believe in sin
But if Jesus came to your church, would they actually let Him in?
See, remember He was called a glutton and a drunkard by religious men
But the Son of God never supports self-righteousness
— not now, not then

Now back to the point — one thing is vital to mention
How Jesus and religion are on opposite spectrums
See, one's the work of God, but one's a man-made invention
See, one is the cure, but the other's the infection

Poem

See, because religion says "do"; Jesus says "done"
Religion says "slave"; Jesus says "son"
Religion puts you in bondage, while Jesus sets you free
Religion makes you blind, but Jesus makes you see
And that's why religion and Jesus are two different clans

Religion is man searching for God; Christianity is
God searching for man
Which is why salvation is freely mine, and forgiveness is my own
Not based on my merits, but Jesus' obedience alone
Because He took the crown of thorns, and the blood dripped down His face
He took what we all deserved — I guess that's why you call it grace
And while being murdered, He yelled,
"Father, forgive them; they know not what they do."
Because when He was dangling on that cross,
He was thinking of you
And He absorbed all your sin, and He buried it in the tomb
Which is why I'm kneeling at the cross, saying,
"Come on, there's room"
So for religion — no, I hate it; in fact I literally resent it
Because when Jesus said, "It is finished," I believe He meant it

----

ENDNOTES:

1. Why I Hate Religion but Love Jesus, by Jefferson Bethke; https://
   genius.com/Jefferson-bethke-why-i-hate-religion-but-love-jesus-
   annotated

1 ❖

The Deterioration of the Church

Truth for the Journey
1st July 2021 – Prophetic Word

Jesus is Lord

For some time, I've been concerned for the Church and its leaders. It's important first of all to respect everyone, and not to undermine the committed relationships that one has made, nor usurp positions of authority or responsibility.

I also, of course, respect denominational groups and continue to work with everyone, where I possibly can. In Romans 12:16-18 in the Amplified it emphasises clearly that we are to **live in harmony with one another.**

And then it goes on to say, "Do not be haughty [conceited, self-important, exclusive], but associate with humble people [those with a realistic self-view]. **Do not overestimate yourself.** Never repay anyone evil for evil. Take thought for what is right and gracious and proper in the sight of everyone. **If possible, as far as it depends on you, live at peace with everyone."**

Division or Self-Preservation

Within the Church, of course, there is much diversity. But diversity was never meant to bring division or self-preservation, *(certainly where culture is concerned)*. It's true to say that I am English and white by birth, but I progressed to Kingdom status, and am now seated with Christ.

> *There is neither Jew nor Gentile, neither slave nor free, nor is there male and female, for **you are all one in Christ Jesus.***
>
> *(Galatians 3:28)*

We are all ONE, yet the Church has seemingly developed into a largely divided BLACK or WHITE entity! Representing, for the most part, traditions and culture. We've moved away from the bible and have become traditional or at best RELIGIOUS. We also see ministers promoting themselves above their congregations, by wearing such ostentatious **religious garments,** (meaning "grandiose" and "pretentious"), which only serves towards "self-aggrandisement."

Please let me say this, *"We put no stumbling block in any-one's path, so that our ministry will not be discredited. Rather, as servants of God we commend ourselves in every way"* (2 Corinthians

6:3). I was ordained a Bishop in Uganda overseeing 300 churches back in 2004 *(I have personally travelled to over 50 countries, written over 80 books, ordained over 500 ministers through CFE, and trained hundreds of Pastors through our global network of university campuses and correspondence courses of LICU)*, and my message is still the same, Apostles need to be restored, not Bishops.

Religious people have a way of taking what is scriptural, sacred and workable and converting it into a lifeless religious form and a pyramid hierarchal structure that restricts God's purpose and brings bondage to His people.

Monarchical Bishops

When the Church becomes more structural than spiritual, it becomes petrified wood instead of a fruitful growing tree with the sap flowing. When it becomes more spiritual than structural, it becomes like dissipating and destructive floodwaters without any control or order.

For this reason, both Apostles and Prophets must be prominent and coequal in laying the foundation for the Church. No church will have a balanced and proper foundation and function without the ministry of both Apostles and Prophets.[1]

In fact we need all Five Gifts!

It was he who gave some to be apostles, some to be prophets, some to be evangelists, and some to be pastors and teachers, to prepare God's people for works of service, so that the body of Christ may be built up until we all reach unity in the faith and in the knowledge of the Son of God and become mature, attaining to the whole measure of the fullness of Christ.

(Ephesians 4:11-13)

There is nothing in this system, which corresponds exactly to the modern diocese episcopate; Bishops, when they are mentioned *(Philippians 1:1)* are from a board of local congregational officers and the position occupied by Timothy and Titus is that of Paul's personal lieutenants in his missionary work. It seems most likely that he was then specially designated with the title of Bishop; but even when the monarchical Bishop appears in the letters of Ignatius, he is still the Pastor of a single congregation.

The word **episkopos** occurs five times in the NT: once of Christ *(1 Peter 2:25)* and in four places of "Bishops" or **"Overseers" in local churches** *(Acts 20:28; Philippians 1:1; 1 Timothy 3:2; Titus 1:7)*. The verb **episkopeo** occurs in Hebrews 12:15 *("watching")* and *(in some NT MSS)* 1 Peter 5:2 *("exercising the oversight")*.[2]

Pyramid Papal System

A Bishop may be the Senior Pastor of a local church, or the apostolic-Prophet or prophetic-Apostle over several ministers and churches. It is not necessarily a fivefold calling, but an administrative office that is given by others and not by oneself.

I am scripturally convinced that the use of the title "Bishop" is not wrong if the person bearing the title meets its qualifications and if the motive and purpose for its usage are according to Biblical principles. **But if the office of Bishop develops into a pyramid papal system** *[man made]* as it did during the deterioration of the Church, then it becomes wrong.[3]

We are meant to be making disciples for Jesus! **When was the last time you saw Jesus** *(within this New Covenant of better things),* **dress up like a Pharisee, in such religious garb?**

PLEASE, let somebody, SOMEBODY out there show me ONE SCRIPTURE in the New Testament, where it says that we should dress with such religious clothing, pomp and ceremony? My bible tells me that I am to forsake all for the sake of Christ.

But whatever former things were gains to me [as I thought then], these things [once regarded as advancements in merit] I have come to consider as loss [absolutely worthless] for the sake of Christ [and the purpose which He has given my life].

But more than that, I count everything as loss compared to the priceless privilege and supreme advantage of knowing Christ Jesus my Lord [and of growing more deeply and thoroughly acquainted with Him — a joy unequaled].

For His sake I have lost everything, and I consider it all garbage, so that I may gain Christ, and may be found in Him [believing and relying on Him], not having any righteousness of my own derived from [my obedience to] the Law and its rituals, but

[possessing] that [genuine righteousness] which comes through faith in Christ, the righteousness which comes from God on the basis of faith.

(Philippians 3:7-9 AMP)

I will follow up this letter of deep concern...

From my desk,
Dr Alan

ENDNOTES:

1. Taken from "Apostles Prophets and the Coming Moves of God" by Dr Bill Hamon, page 175, Copyright © 1997, Published by Destiny Image Publishers USA

2. Taken from "Apostles, Can the Church Survive Without Them?" by Dr Alan Pateman, page 25-26, Copyright © 2012, Published by APMI Publications; see also "The Age of Apostolic Apostleship, Complete Series" by Dr Alan Pateman, Copyright © 2017, Published by APMI Publications

3. Taken from "Apostles Prophets and the Coming Moves of God" by Dr Bill Hamon, page 178, Copyright © 1997, Published by Destiny Image Publishers USA

4. This "Truth for the Journey" has been taken from: https://watchersofthe4kings.com

5. Scripture quotations marked AMP are taken from the Amplified® Bible, Copyright © 2015 by The Lockman Foundation. Used by permission. (www.Lockman.org)

2❖

Unscriptural Heights

Truth for the Journey
16th July 2021 – Deep Concern

Massive Feedback

Since my last letter of *Deep Concern* to the Church, *(1st July 2021)* regarding the Body of Christ and its leadership, which I entitled "We are Bigger than Religion," I've received massive feedback, coming from different platforms. It has been overwhelmingly positive, thus far.

In this letter, let's start by being mindful that Christ's Commission to the Church remains as it has always been, to the entire world. People, we cannot be duped. There is nothing racist about the gospel message. "WHOLE WORLD… ALL NATIONS" is a pretty inclusive concept!

This gospel of the kingdom will be preached in the whole world as a testimony to all nations, and then the end will come.

(Matthew 24:14)

Our Concern is the Kingdom

The Kingdom of God, in Christianity generally refers to the spiritual realm over which God reigns as King and the fulfilment of God's will, on earth. The phrase is primarily used by Jesus in the first three Gospels and is generally considered to be the central theme of Jesus' teaching in the New Testament.

Remember, we are called to preach the KINGDOM, and as we discovered in my last letter, the Kingdom of God, is not about colour or culture at all. Rather, we're instructed scripturally to be TRANSFORMED BY THE RENEWING OF OUR MINDS. We are told to put on the MIND OF CHRIST, *(Romans 12:2; 1 Corinthians 2:13-16; 2 Timothy 1:7)*.

Therefore, if our message is more comfortable with traditions and culture, or a black or white message, then we've already succumbed to a *cult or sect-like mentality.*

Thus you nullify the word of God by your tradition that you have handed down. And you do many things like that.
(Mark 7:13)

The Definition of a Cult

According to various dictionaries online, *the definition of a cult* is as follows: "A religion or religious sect generally considered to be extremist or false, with its followers often living in an unconventional manner under the guidance of an authoritarian, charismatic leader..." "Obsessive, especially faddish, devotion to *or veneration for a person, principle, or thing.*"

"A system of intense *religious veneration of a particular person, idea,* or *object,* especially one considered spurious or irrational by traditional religious bodies. A group of people with a religious, philosophical or *cultural identity* sometimes viewed as a sect, often existing on the margins of society or exploitative towards its members."[1]

The Merriam Webster Dictionary says, *the definition of a sect is: "A group adhering to a distinctive doctrine or to a leader* – a party or a faction." "A dissenting or schismatic religious body especially: one regarded as extreme or heretical. A religious denomination."[2]

Critical Race Theory

Then of course there is a question, "Has Critical Race Theory successfully infiltrated the Body of Christ?" *(Which is currently creating a political storm in the USA).*

The entire social justice warrior message seems very Christian indeed, but not so fast:

> Critical race theory is absolutely contrary to Christianity...
> The idea that people would be oppressors based solely on their ethnicity... would be completely at odds with the scriptures.
>
> -- *Voddie Baucham Jr.*

Baucham, who formerly pastored at Grace Family Baptist Church in Houston and now serves as the dean of theology at African Christian University in Zambia, says, "The entire premise of critical race theory is flawed..." **He said that it's illogical to pin one's goodness — or lack of it — on race.** "The idea that white people are incapable of righteous actions [sic] on race, again, you just can't get there from here... So, the fundamental presuppositions of this are at odds... with rational thinking."[3]

A Dangerous Uptick in Self Promotion

The other area where we're seeing a great uptick is the area of self-promotion. Specifically, we're seeing more and more, certain individuals within church leadership that are promoting themselves to a status that's not even scriptural.

As I've already previously stated, I am not against Bishops. A Bishop is purely an "Overseer," "an Elder," "a pillar" and "an administrator" of the local church. Plus, Paul taught and demonstrated that the church was not complete until Elders *(plural)* were installed *(Acts 14:23)*.

Once again, let it be very clear, that all Bishops are Elders and pillars in the local church. Remembering that the position of the Bishop *(Elder)* is an office to administrate the affairs of the church. On the other hand, he or she may be gifted in a number of different ways, pastoral, teaching, etc. but remember he or she is always a pillar in the local church.

Don't forget that I too, am an ordained Bishop. Bishop Charles Kiwanuka Kaisaali, of Power Centre Church Entebbe,

Uganda back in 2004, ordained me. But I did not lose sight of what that actually meant; that we are "Overseers" *(please refer to my first letter for clarity)*.

However, this doesn't mean to say that a Bishop is apostolic *(apostolic means a "sent one")*, not at all. Remember, it's the Apostles and Prophets who lay the foundations of the Church not Bishops.

Unscriptural Heights

Bishops are being raised up to unscriptural heights, developing themselves into **a papal type system,** Pope-like structure, patterned on the Catholic Church. This happened during the deterioration of the church, *(during the dark ages)*. Today however, it seems that much of the church has taken on the mantel *(dogma - philosophy)* of the Catholic Church!

Let me just say, the Catholic Church has not long ago, "officially accepted" that salvation is by grace and not by works. *(Seriously, it's only been within the last 20 or 30 years approximately)*.

> *For it is by grace you have been saved, through faith – and this is not from yourselves, it is the gift of God –* ***not by works,*** *so that no one can boast.*
>
> *(Ephesians 2:8-9)*

So, they're a bit late to the party, considering **Martin Luther** nailed his 95 theses to the door of the castle church in Wittenberg, over five hundred years ago, on Oct. 31, 1517, **which ignited a religious revolution.**

Just for your own interest, I believe that when the antichrist reveals himself *(2 Thessalonians 2:4)*, **the acting Catholic Pope at that time will then come alongside the antichrist as the false prophet.**

Alongside the Antichrist

"In Revelation 19:11, Christ appears on a white horse to rule as King of kings and Lord of lords. But stubborn and rebellious to the end, the Antichrist insists any enemy, including Christ, will never defeat him. However, this time he is wrong, because Christ destroys him with the brightness of His coming *(2 Thessalonians 2:8)*. Christ then takes the global dictator—along with the false prophet who headed up the world church—and casts them both into a lake of fire *(Revelation 19:20)*.

A thousand years later, when Satan is thrown into that same lake of fire, the beast and the false prophet still exist, suffering the torment of hell forever and ever *(Revelation 20:10)*."[4]

He'll be the overseer over all religions that have been accepted in association or affiliation by the Catholic Church. Remembering that the current Pope is already embracing ALL religions.

From my desk,
...There is more to come!

Dr Alan

ENDNOTES:

1. https://www.wordnik.com/words/cult; From The American Heritage® Dictionary of the English Language, 5th Edition

2. https://www.merriam-webster.com/dictionary/sect

3. https://www.dailysignal.com/2021/06/18/critical-race-theory-is-antithetical-to-christianity-black-pastor-says/

4. "Millennium: Beginning or End?" by Jack Van Impe, page 67, Copyright © 1999 Jack Van Impe Ministries; Published by Word Publishing, a unit of Thomas Nelson, Inc. USA

5. This "Truth for the Journey" has been taken from: https://watchersofthe4kings.com

3 ❖

Power or Influence

Truth for the Journey
6th August 2021 – Prophetic Letter

Jesus Himself Chose Power not Influence

For ye see your calling, brethren, how that **not many wise men after the flesh, not many mighty, not many noble, are called:** But God hath chosen the foolish things of the world to confound the wise; and God hath chosen the weak things of the world to confound the things which are mighty *(1 Corinthians 1:26-27 KJV).*

Let's jump right into this Truth for the Journey and say, God wants us to choose power over influence. Why? Because when we have power, this proves that we have influence with God! On the flipside however, courting the influence of men, always causes us to lose influence with God. If we seek influence, we will not automatically have the power of God. That's the cost. Influence with men vs. influence with God. **One procures power from earth; the other procures power from heaven.**

Power for Revival

When one moves in the power of God, i.e. blind eyes be opened, the lame walk and the dead are raised, influence will be at your door!

To solidify my point, I'll refer to a favourite book of mine, written by Duncan Campbell, which is filled with golden nuggets of revelation and is entitled, "The Price and Power of Revival."[1]

Concerning power versus influence, Duncan wrote: "The Apostles were not men of influence, *'not many mighty, not many noble.'* Oh no, the Master Himself did not choose to be a man of influence. 'He made Himself of no reputation' *(Philippians 2:7)*, all of which is equal to saying that God chose power rather than influence."

Listen to what Duncan says next: "I sometimes think of Paul and Silas… in Philippi. Why? They had not enough influence to keep them out of prison, but possessed of the power of God in such a manner that their prayers in prison shook the whole prison to its very foundations. **Not influence, but power.**"

Considering that Duncan first published this book back in 1956, it still reads like it had been written today. He continues, "Oh, that the Church today, in our congregations and in our pulpits, would re-discover this truth and get back to the place of God realisation, to the place of power. **I want to say further that we should seek power even at the expense of influence.**

What do I mean by that? I mean this: I hear people say today, these are different days from the days of the 1895 Revival or the Welsh Revival *(1904);* **we must be tolerant and we must try to accommodate.** In order to do that it is necessary at times to **lower our standard** and see the co-operation of those who do not accept the position that we hold relative to evangelical truth." *(Sound familiar? It's exactly what we face today).*

The Secret to Power - Separation

Duncan goes on to say, **"The secret of power is separation from all that is unclean, for me there is nothing so unclean as the liberal views held by some today...** I am stating what to me is a deep-seated conviction: 'Come out from among them and be ye separate...'"

> *"Therefore, **come out from them and be separate,** says the Lord. Touch no unclean thing, and I will receive you."* And, *"I will be a Father to you, and you will be my sons and daughters, says the Lord Almighty."*
> *(2 Corinthians 6:17-18)*

"Yes, **we must seek power even at the expense of influence.** Think again of the great Apostle Paul. What an opportunity he had of gaining influence with Felix, had he but flattered him a little in his sin, he could have made a great impression, and I believe he could have got a handsome donation for his missionary effort by being tolerant, by accommodating the situation.

> *Away with your milk and water preaching of the love of Christ that has no holiness or moral discrimination in it, away with the preaching a Christ not crucified for sin.*
>   *-- Charles Finney*

Paul chose power before influence... on the solid ground of separation unto God. Now the person who will take his stand on that ground, will not be popular, he will not be popular with some preachers of today who declare that we must soft-pedal in order to capture and captivate...

> *Bring me a God all mercy but not just, bring me a God all love but not righteous, and I will have no scruples in calling Him an idiot of your imagination.*
>   *-- Unknown"*

Now, let me clarify, that influence is not all bad, it depends how one procures it. We must seek the influence that comes with the power of God and not power that comes with having influence with men alone.

Where was the Power of the Church during Covid-19?

In our latest conversations the emphasis has been on the creeping dogma within the Pentecostal church, when really our emphasis aught always to be the preaching of the good news, laying hands on the sick and casting out demons and raising the dead. The problem is this: to fulfil the commission on the church takes power *(Matthew 28:18 says: "All power in heaven and on earth has been given to me." Some translations use the word "authority").* **Influence without power is as useless as salt-less salt!**

The question must be: *If the church is powerless in the face of issues like Covid-19 – because we are too internally fixated on our own identity crises – then what's the point of us? What good is our influence, if we have lost it both with men and with God?*

The church has no power, to a great extent. As we've seen in recent times, when Covid-19 approached the doors of our churches and closed them tight! Consequently, for us to get distracted *(religious and goofy)* at a time like this – which is an unprecedented time in history – it's a big mistake.

I implore the Pentecostal church *(and any other groups that may be falling for this religion of mixtures)*, not to allow such traditions and dogmas to "make the word of God of none effect" *(Mark 7:13 KJV).*

You cannot have it both ways, to criticize the Catholic Church and yet become the Catholic Church.

Birthing a Spiritual Mule!

I won't digress from our central theme of power versus influence, but will sure it up with scriptural evidence that spiritual mixtures don't please God. In the same sense that the mating of a donkey with a horse births a sterile mule, likewise the wrong spiritual mixtures create the same... *to be sterile is to be powerless.*

Here are some references found in the Old Testament *(as a type and a shadow)* to substantiate God's utter disdain of spiritual mixtures:

> *You shall not let your cattle breed with a different kind. You shall not sow your field with two kinds of seed, nor shall you wear a garment of cloth made of two kinds of material.*
> *(Leviticus 19:19 ESV)*

> *You shall not wear cloth of wool and linen mixed together.*
> *(Deuteronomy 22:11 ESV)*

> *You shall not sow your vineyard with two kinds of seed, lest the whole yield be forfeited, the crop that you have sown and the yield of the vineyard.*
> *(Deuteronomy 22:9 ESV)*

> *A woman shall not wear a man's garment, nor shall a man put on a woman's cloak, for whoever does these things is an abomination to the Lord your God.*
> *(Deuteronomy 22:5 ESV)*

Be Not Unequally Yoked

Correspondingly, **the New Testament continues this theme** of spiritual mixtures, with perhaps the most notable being in Matthew 13:29-30, concerning the wheat and the tares, which describes the final separation that will occur at judgment.

Mixtures exist between truth and error, light and darkness, or even trying to mix the Holy Spirit with other spirits *(unclean/unholy)*. Incidentally the Holy Spirit will not cohabit, not even with a church-spirit *(religious)*. Don't forget how hotly Jesus exhibited His displeasure towards them *(the religious elite)*, calling them out as "vipers" and as the "blind leading the blind." Even the reference in James 3:15 describes the spiritual decline from, earthly to soulish, to demonic.

Therefore, I strongly maintain, that we must not become spiritually incapacitated, at a time like this, caught in the midst of odd spiritual permutations. What then is the solution? We must be able to recognise the Holy Spirit and walk in Him *(Galatians 5:25-26)*.

But let me be crystal clear. This is not about a lack of diversity or racism. Instead what the scriptures are referring to is the mixture of truth and error:

> ***Be ye not unequally yoked*** *together with unbelievers: for what fellowship hath righteousness with unrighteousness? and what communion hath light with darkness? And what concord hath Christ with Belial? or what part hath he that believeth with an infidel? And what agreement hath the temple of God with idols?*
>
> *For ye are the temple of the living God; as God hath said, I will dwell in them, and walk in them; and I will be their God, and they shall be my people...*
> *(2 Corinthians 6:14-17 KJV)*

Finally, and possibly the most famous reference, is Christ's own disgust with the mixture of faith and unbelief *(obedience and disobedience)*, declaring it vomit inducing! "I know your works. You are neither cold with apathy nor hot with passion [but mixed]. It would be better if you were one or the other, but you are neither. So because you are lukewarm, neither cold nor hot, I will vomit you out of My Mouth" *(Revelation 3:15-16 VOICE [emphasis added]).*

Think about it, we cannot be both dead and alive, at the same time. Clearly we must be one or the other, "…therefore choose life" *(Deuteronomy 30:19).*

Question: *What makes us think, that the Holy Spirit wants to reside with a religious spirit, all of a sudden? How does that fit? It won't end well.*

This is our Influence and has always been our Power

There shall no evil befall thee, neither shall any plague come nigh thy dwelling.

(Psalm 91:10 KJV)

Even in a time of disaster, with thousands and thousands being killed, you will remain unscathed and unharmed… When we live our lives within the shadow of God Most High, our secret hiding place, we will always be shielded from harm. **How then could evil prevail against us or disease infect us?**

(Psalm 91:7,9 TPT)

For nation shall rise against nation, and kingdom against kingdom: and there shall be famines, and **pestilences,** *and earthquakes, in divers places… All these are the beginning of sorrows… But* **he that shall endure unto the end, the same shall be saved.**

(Matthew 24:7-8,13 KJV)

Amen

Church, come alive!
Let's choose Power; influence will follow!
Dr Alan

ENDNOTES:

1. "The Price and Power of Revival" by Duncan Campbell, Published in 1956 by Parry Jackman, in London UK

2. This "Truth for the Journey" has been taken from: https://watchersofthe4kings.com

3. Scripture references marked ESV are from the ESV® Bible (The Holy Bible, English Standard Version®), copyright © 2001 by Crossway, a publishing ministry of Good News Publishers. Used by permission. All rights reserved.

4. Scripture references marked KJV are taken from the King James Version of the Bible.

5. Scripture quotations marked TPT are from The Passion Translation®. Copyright © 2017, 2018 by Passion & Fire Ministries, Inc. Used by permission. All rights reserved. ThePassionTranslation.com

6. Scripture quotations marked VOICE are taken from The Voice™. Copyright © 2008 by Ecclesia Bible Society. Used by permission. All rights reserved.

4❖

Cultural and Religious Appropriation

Truth for the Journey,
16th October 2012 – Religious Dogmas

Aesthetics and Behaviours

In this particular letter to the churches, we're having a conversation about the growing trend amongst Pentecostals Churches regarding the wearing and use of religious garments and paraphernalia, along with the overall adoption of Catholic religious dogmas, in an attempt to gain influence and be taken more seriously.

The question has to be: "Does this weaken or strengthen the Pentecostal Church?"

It once was said, "Whatever you compromise to keep, you'll lose anyway." And in that context, whenever we foolishly attempt to be influential *(in the eyes of the world around us)* at the expense of all else, we subvert our true identity. I see this happening right across the board, but today our conversation centres on the Pentecostal Churches.

Cultural appropriation is frowned on and seen as offensive in today's world, but the same applies to religious appropriation. We cannot take from another's culture and religion *(aesthetics, outward appearance and behaviours)* just to make sense of our own, it doesn't end well.

In plain speech, Pentecostals do not need to become Catholics to be taken seriously, the opposite is true.

> *The mind governed by the flesh is hostile to God; it does not submit to God's law, nor can it do so. Those who are in the realm of the flesh cannot please God.*
> *(Romans 8:7-8)*

So what does all this mean? It means that Pentecostal churches do not need to become religious in order to become acceptable or influential in the religious world, here in Europe or anywhere else. In fact, just by doing so, they actually lose influence and jeopardize even more in the process, I will explain!

Let me just say, that the African Pentecostal church, which I have come to know, love and respect over the last decades of my life, has always been a powerful force to be reckoned with, and I am unwilling to see it weakened.

Losing its authentic identity makes it lose its power; the trade off when trafficking in fleshly influence. Such showboating *(on social media)* with religiosity only weakens the African church, which sadly is a growing and disturbing trend; **I'll say it again, we are bigger than religion.**

We need the African Pentecostal Church to do what it does best, without trading places and becoming unrecognizable! Who needs an African Pentecostal Church that acts like a Catholic High church? No one! In fact it serves no purpose. Rather it's a ditch they've fallen into and must climb out!

There is no competing with the Catholic Church and there should be no metamorphosis either.

You Cannot Seek the Living Amongst the Dead!

In Africa, Catholicism is a massive demographic, infrastructural, and socio-political power. But there it has strong and powerful competitors, including Protestant and Pentecostal churches, Islam, and traditional religions.

In Italy, Catholicism doesn't have significant competitors, other than the Italians' disaffection for the Catholic Church as a religious institution.

In her article entitled **"African Pentecostals in Catholic Europe: An Aesthetic Approach,"** Dr Annalisa Butticci calls this particular subject "Catho-Pentecostal religious aesthetics."[1]

She starts by saying, "In the twenty-first century, more than ever, Africans and Europeans are meeting and living together not only in Africa but also in European cities and societies. According to recent data, in 2016, the majority of new European citizens were from Africa. In countries like Italy, Africans make up 20 percent of the migrant population *(or 1, 047, 229)*. The majority of them come from north Africa *(13 percent)*, followed by sub-Saharan Africa, specifically 2 percent from Senegal, 1.75 percent from Nigeria, and 1 percent from Ghana."

Numbers will have increased since, but the point is still the same, people are moving around and cohabiting like no other time in history, which inevitably has its implications.

Dr Butticci continues, "Among the migrants coming from Nigeria and Ghana, the vast majority are Pentecostals. Their experience as blacks, economic migrants, and non-Catholics in a predominantly white and Catholic society reveals some of the core features of the twenty-first century relationship between Africans and Europeans in European cities and societies. That they are Pentecostals makes them a particularly complicated Christian 'other' that challenges the social and religious order of the Italian society defined by the Roman Catholic ethno-religious power."

And of the African Pentecostals here in Italy she goes on to state: "The history of today's African Pentecostal churches in Italy dates back to the end of the 1980s and the early 1990s, when the first significant migratory movement from West Africa reached Italy. In those years, Nigerian and Ghanaian migrants' departure cities, like Lagos, Benin City, as well as Accra *[capital of Ghana]* and Kumasi, witnessed an impressive growth of Pentecostal mega churches and prayer camps that were attracting members from the historical Protestant and Catholic churches."

A Place of Refuge

In her article she went on to touch such hot topics as xenophobia, racial violence and human trafficking, noting that African Pentecostal churches generally provide a place of refuge for new arrivals, "In these churches, African women and men create a safe space far from the inquisitive and suspicious gaze that they experience in their everyday lives... For these Africans, marginality is not only defined by their migrant condition but by their Pentecostalism: they are not Catholic in a society where Roman Catholicism is a religious and social power."

While the number of people attending Catholic churches here in Italy, is in steady decline, "the Catholic Church remains the expression of a modern ethno-national Italian identity, the custodian of individual and collective memory as well as a religious and social world view." In other words, it represents more than just a religion, but an entire way of life, *(a deeply ingrained culture)*.

She adds, "Catholic religious aesthetics in Italy are indeed overwhelming and deeply ingrained in Italian social life. Pentecostals observe the spectacle of Catholic aesthetics and power and often **shake their heads and react in disgust,** for example at the remains of human bodies that Catholics venerate as relics."

In fact our youngest daughter was quite taken-aback at the sight of dead saints left on display! She thought it quite barbaric. But she was much too young to understand the wider issues!

Religious Osmosis

Does that mean, those who shake their heads in disgust eventually become the very thing they claim to disapprove of? *(The frog has slowly been boiling in water! Cultural and religious osmosis implies that which is dominant and pervasive, prevails).*

However, Dr Butticci continues by saying, "Intriguingly, although African Pentecostals reject Roman Catholicism as a religion and as the ethno-religious principle that governs the Italian nation state, **they nonetheless appropriate and manipulate Roman Catholic aesthetic power for their own spiritual ends...** In African Pentecostal churches in Italy, one can observe what I call a surprising transcultural 'Catho-Pentecostal' visual and material culture. For instance, one can see African Pentecostals wearing religious robes that seem strikingly similar to Catholics' vestments.

Such cases are particularly noticeable when female Pastors use Catholic-style robes, as in the case of an iconic female Ghanaian Bishop named Diana. She claims to be the first female African ordained as a Bishop in Europe. She is particularly known in Italy for her work with young Nigerian and Ghanaian girls and for campaigning tirelessly for the ordination of female Pastors and Bishops, ordination that, she says, will encourage women to take the right path and bring honor and dignity to African women in Italy.

After her own ordination in Ghana, Bishop Diana started ordaining women, and greatly increased the number of women Pastors in Italy. **Her very presence and appearance**

as a black female and religious leader, often dressed in Catholic robes, in a Catholic country where women have no access to priesthood, is an intriguing religious and social statement."

Citing an interview with Bishop Diana, as part of a documentary called, "Enlarging the Kingdom: African Pentecostals in Italy," Butticci adds: "Her style is not mere provocation but the aesthetic form of her political imagination.

Bishop Diana dresses like a Catholic cardinal: she wears a black robe with a red cincture, and high-heeled red stiletto shoes. Adorned in her regalia, she proudly walks down the street, in her black-and-red robe looking like an otherworldly apparition: a black female Catholic cardinal walking down an Italian street."

Butticci mentioned also the use of religious imagery, such as "altar decorations with images of Jesus, like the Transfiguration of Christ of Raffaello Sarti" and the use of holy water and other rituals, concluding with this, **"Yet what one might think could connect Catholics and Pentecostals actually only pushes them further apart and increasingly excludes them."**

"In Italy, Pentecostals are not even recognized as legitimate religious authorities and so it seems particularly unlikely that they could subvert the Catholic aesthetic order."

It seems to me that people are sold out seeking influence rather than God's Power!

If you want an identity then seek the presence of His Holy Spirit, then go and **make disciples of Jesus** in all nations, Not Your Self, Group, Assembly or Church.

Dr Alan

ENDNOTES:

1. **Annalisa Butticci** is currently Assistant Professor of Social Anthropology at Utrecht University in the Netherlands. Her areas of research include religious practices and aesthetics, material and visual culture of religions, religions and societies of West Africa, African Diasporas, interreligious and interracial relations, Roman Catholicism and Pentecostalism(s), visual and multimedia studies, and oral history and life stories. She has conducted extensive research in Italy, Nigeria, Ghana, and the US. Her latest book "African Pentecostals in Catholic Europe: The Politics of Presence in the Twenty-First Century" *(Harvard University Press, 2016)* was awarded honorable mention by the 2017 Clifford Geertz Prize committee in recognition of its contribution to the anthropological study of religion.

   She is the co-director of the film/documentary "Enlarging the Kingdom. African Pentecostalism in Italy" *(28min)*, editor of the photographic catalogue "Na God. Aesthetics of African Charismatic Power" *(2013)*, curator of several photographic and multimedia exhibitions, and author of articles published in scientific journals and edited volumes. She received her MA in Political Science from the University of Padua, a post master degree in Gender Studies from the University of Bologna, and a PhD from the Catholic University of Milan, Italy.

   Published on March 1, 2018; https://www.europenowjournal. org/2018/02/28/africans-pentecostals-in-catholic-europe-an-aesthetic-approach/

   This is part of a special feature, Beyond Eurafrica: Encounters in a Globalized World. http://councilforeuropeanstudies.org/

2. This "Truth for the Journey" has been taken from: https:// watchersofthe4kings.com

5❖

The Pyramid-Hierarchal Structure

Truth for the Journey
16th October 2019 – Papal Religious Structure

Historical Background

In the secular world, any talk of pyramidal structures, quickly refers to such things as the dreaded Ponzi scheme or one the many variants of the same idea *(fraudulent investment scheme)*. However, in the religious world, it largely points to the Catholic Church. In the scriptures there's no better example of this pyramid structure than the tower of babel, *(found in Genesis 11:1-9)*.

Let me interject, that wherever the Kingdom of God is involved, it's less about *taking* control and more about *giving* it, *(lifting up the Body of Christ; the prophetic message is "Let My People Go")*. It's about enhancing others and making disciples, which makes it more of an inverted pyramid ["V"]. This is when leadership gets underneath the church to raise it up, rather than dominating it.

Leadership is then at the bottom, rather than on the top. Mark 9:35 says, "If any man desire to be first, the same shall be last of all, and servant of all" *(KJV)*. And being in service to God, is not a means of making money *(see 1 Timothy 6:5-10 KJV)*.

> *...men of corrupt minds, and destitute of the truth,* **supposing that gain is godliness...**
> (1 Timothy 6:5 KJV)

> *They are always making trouble, because they are people whose thinking has been confused. They have lost their understanding of the truth.* **They think that devotion to God is a way to get rich.**
> (1 Timothy 6:5 ERV)

True **ministry is not a lucrative career option.** It's tough dealing with sin and the real issues of the human soul. It's messy, just like washing feet! We help them get clean; it can be a thankless vocation. After all it's a disturbing message that we preach!

> *This is what our age needs, not an easy-moving message, the sort that makes the hearer feel all nice inside, but a message profoundly disturbing. We have been far too afraid of disturbing people,* **but the Holy Spirit will**

have nothing to do with a message or with a minister who is afraid of disturbing.

*You might as well expect a surgeon to give place to a quack who claims to be able to do the job with some sweet tasting drug, **as expect the Holy Spirit to agree that the tragic plight of human souls today can be met by soft and easy words. Calvary was anything but nice to look at, blood-soaked beams of wood, a bruised and bleeding body, not nice to look upon.***

*But then **Jesus was not dealing with a nice thing; He was dealing with the sin of the world** that is what we are called upon to deal with today. Soft and easy words, soft-pedalling will never meet the need.*

-- Rev. Robert Barr, B.D.,
Presbyterian Church South Africa

"Holier Than Thou"

Some ministers who are playing dress up think that by wearing such religious garb (*garments, robes and vestments*), they can impose "holier than thou" airs and graces upon their congregants. But not so fast! As we have all seen in the high profile cases and legal dramas that unfolded over recent decades involving the Roman Catholic Church and their proven cover up of the countless priests who were long-standing active paedophiles, who defiled a generation of children.

*Stand by thyself, come not near to me; **for I am holier than thou.***

(Isaiah 65:5 KJV)

Such individuals, who clearly abused their position, were also dressed up, according to the hierarchal rank within the church. However, it was clear for all to see that **their garments were not equal to a life of holiness.** It amounted to little more than religious theatre, providing a façade for their crimes to stay in the shade, for decades.

It is an open secret *(that's evolved into common knowledge)* that prostitution, homosexuality and pornography has long been rife within the Ministry or Priesthood.

Official statistics exist that specifically reveal the consumption of pornography by Conservatives, Christians, Pastors and churchgoers. Take for instance the Promise Keepers survey that was conducted at one of their stadium events, which revealed how over 50% of the men in attendance had viewed pornography within one week of attending the event!

(Promise Keepers is a large Men's ministry in America, whose slogan is: "Men of Integrity").

- 51% of Pastors say cyber-porn is a possible temptation. 37% say it is a current struggle *(Christianity Today, Leadership Survey, 12/2002).*

- Over half of evangelical Pastors admit to viewing pornography in the past year.

- Roger Charman of Focus on the Family's Pastoral Ministries reports that approximately 20 percent of the calls received on their Pastoral Care Line are for help with issues such as pornography and compulsive sexual behaviour.

- In a 2000 Christianity Today survey, 33% of clergy admitted to having visited a sexually explicit web site. Of those who had visited a porn site, 53% had visited such sites "a few times" in the past year and 18% visit sexually explicit sites between a couple of times a month and more than once a week.

- 29% of born again adults in the US feel it is "morally acceptable" to view movies with explicit sexual behaviour *(The Barna Group)*.

- 57% of Pastors say that addiction to pornography is the most sexually damaging issue to their congregation *(Christians and Sex, Leadership Journal Survey, March 2005)*.

We could go on and on with such statistics but already it's very evident that in general society's standards of morality are slipping to an all time low and by all indications will continue in a pattern of steady decline.

As Christians we are not exempt from such temptations, something that has been openly proven, time and again. Sadly even our moral compass is slipping. Evidently, every one of us is capable of being vehemently outraged by the very things we're struggling with ourselves! Only the spiritually strong will survive, those who live by faith and not by sight.

We live in a particular time in history, where life as we know it is being sexually super charged. This is something that is totally premeditated from the devil's point of view and something that we cannot treat casually – as scripture warns: *"If the righteous scarcely be saved, where shall the ungodly and the sinner appear?" (1 Peter 4:18)* Also James 1:27 warns us to keep *"unspotted from the world."* And 1 Timothy 5:22 adds, *"...keep thyself pure."*

> *The temptation to give in to evil comes from us and only us. We have no one to blame but the leering, seducing flare-up of our own lusts...*
>
> *(James 1:14 MSG)*

To the pure all things are pure, nevertheless we must relentlessly pursue purity and even militantly keep ourselves pure. Not out of religious piety but motivated from a true desire from genuine godliness. Even though the world around us no longer recognises purity as a virtue or desirable quality to be acquired.[1]

Historically, as had been widely documented, immorality has often been kept conveniently hidden beneath the "cloth." Not to mention the many pompous titles such as, "Your Holiness," titles that are not even worthy of the holders. So let's not make any further mockery of these things, considering scripture already tells us that our righteousness is as filthy rags *(Isaiah 64:6)*.

And although the Old Testament records God as saying, "Be holy as I am holy" *(Leviticus 11:44-45)*, Jesus said of Himself in the New Testament, "Why do you call me good? No one is good except God alone" *(Mark 10:18)* and Peter later said, "...there is no other name under heaven given to mankind by which we must be saved" *(Acts 4:12)*.

None other than Christ Himself is Holy, so as individuals or even as ministers, we must endeavour to "take up our cross daily" *(Luke 9:23)*. Rather it's as we yield to His Spirit of Holiness within, that we find ourselves living in the true beauty of holiness. Such a life is impossible to achieve in the flesh or carnal nature *(Galatians 5:19-21)*.

Both John the Baptist and Jesus targeted the religious leaders of the day for their evident hypocrisy, calling them snakes *(Matthew 23:33)* and blind guides who lead the blind *(Matthew 15:14)*.

Evidently then, yielding to a religious mind-set is deceptive because it is blind to the fact that only God Himself is holy. Blind religion can only produce blindness in others. Such deception *(via false teaching)* is dangerous because "…both will fall into a pit" *(Matthew 15:14b)*.

The Historical Development of the Title "Bishop"

I have taken some helpful excerpts from Bill Hamon's book: **"Apostles Prophets and the Coming Moves of God."** This book is an excellent resource for the hungry disciple of Christ, its message is timeless and I highly recommend it.[2]

"After an initial three hundred years of rejection and persecution by Judaism and the nations of the world, Christianity became an accepted religion within the Roman Empire. This change was made law by the Roman Emperor Constantine, who issued an 'Edict of Toleration' in AD313 allowing Christianity to function publically the same as any other religion or secular society.

Christian churches moved from being underground to government recognized. Christians were allowed citizenship and the right to hold political offices. Within a few years hundreds of churches were built throughout the Roman Empire and other parts of the world. Local congregations began to relate to certain trans-local leaders, and **some leaders began to press for position and control.**

Centralization of Control

At the close of what fundamentalist church historians call the *(first)* Apostolic Age, churches were independent of each other, shepherded by the fivefold ministries, who were generally called Pastors or Elders. The main leader or Senior Pastor came to be called 'Bishop,' which means 'Overseer.' Gradually, the jurisdiction of the Bishop came to include neighbouring churches in the other towns.

Bishop Calixtus *(a Bishop of Rome, AD217-222)* was the first to base his claim to authority on Matthew 16:18.

And I tell you that you are Peter, and on this rock I will build my church, and the gates of Hades will not overcome it.

Note: *Jesus in reference to this revelation was referring to the Rhema, and that He would build His church on His Rhema word.*

The great theologian Tertullian of Carthage called Calixtus a usurper in speaking as if he were the 'Bishop of Bishops.' When Constantine called the council of Nicea in AD325 and presided over the first worldwide council of churches, he accorded the Bishops of Alexandria and Antioch full jurisdiction over their provinces, as the Roman Bishop had over his.

By the end of the 4th century, the eastern Bishops had come to be called 'patriarchs.' They were of equal authority, each having full control of his own province. The five Bishops/Patriarchs who dominated Christendom at the time were headquartered in Rome, Constantinople, Antioch, Jerusalem and Alexandria.

After the division of the Roman Empire into East and West, the struggle for the leadership of Christendom was between Rome *(Roman Catholics)* and Constantinople *(Eastern Orthodox)*.

Development of the One-Man Rule Papal Religious Structure

In the earlier centuries of the Church the Bishops came to be affectionately addressed as 'papa' *(father)*, which gave rise to the word 'Pope.' About the year AD500, 'papa' began to be restricted in its use by the local Bishops, and the title was eventually reserved exclusively for the Bishop of Rome.

Over the centuries the word came to mean 'universal Bishop.' The idea that the Bishop of Rome should have authority over the whole Church grew slowly and was bitterly contested. By the middle of the Dark Ages, the papal reign of one-man rule had reached a position of supreme power and international jurisdiction.

Prophets and Apostles
Need to be Restored Not Bishops

Religious people have a way of taking what is scriptural, sacred and workable and converting it into a lifeless religious form and a pyramid hierarchal structure that restricts God's purpose and brings bondage to His people. When the Church becomes more structural than spiritual, it becomes petrified wood instead of a fruitful growing tree with the sap flowing. When it becomes more spiritual than structural, it becomes like dissipating and destructive floodwaters without any control or order.

Let me say it again, both Apostles and Prophets must be prominent and coequal in laying the foundation for the Church. No church will have a balanced and proper foundation and function without the ministry of both Apostles and Prophets.

If a church is built with the ministry of the Apostle alone, without the Prophet ministry, it may become so doctrinally structured and ordered that it becomes lifeless and formal without the fiery flow of praise and power.

If the Prophet alone, without the ministry of the Apostle, builds the church the people may become so spiritually activated that everyone is a law unto him or herself, and it could lead to fanaticism. **But with the ministry of both the Apostle and Prophet the Church of Jesus Christ will maintain a balance between structure and spirituality, doctrine and demonstration, prophetic perspective and apostolic order.**

Who can be a Bishop?

The word 'Bishop' is a scriptural term *(1 Timothy 3:1; Titus 1:7; 1 Peter 2:25)*. **It can rightly be used as a title that designates a fivefold minister who oversees other people and ministries.** Apostle Peter referred to Jesus as the 'Shepherd' and 'Bishop' of our souls, Some other translations use 'Overseer' instead of 'Bishop,' for they both come from the same root word. Some have made an issue of Charismatic or Prophetic ministers using the title of 'Bishop.'

I will also make an issue of it when ministers teach, that the term 'Bishop,' can only be used by those who wear religious garments developed during the **Dark Ages of the Church.** I have no problem with some ministers wearing robes and clerical collars **as long as they don't portray that the religious garments give them the recognition and authority of a Bishop.**

Part of the Tribe of Levi

This religious protocol was developed from the combination of the Jewish priestly garments and the elaborate robes and ceremonies of kings at the time. **Jesus did not wear priestly garments for He was of the tribe of Judah, not Levi.** The Jews would have stoned Him if He had worn the attire of the high priest, even though in God His position was higher than that of any high priest.

None of the twelve Apostles wore special garments to distinguish them as Apostles. None of them had been trained and ordained as Levitical priests, nor were they of the tribe of Levi or descendants of Aaron. Paul never mentions or implies that he continued to wear robes he wore as a pharisaic doctor of the Law of Moses.

The early Christian Church did not wear special religious garments as the Israeli Aaronic priesthood wore. It had no elaborate hierarchal authority structure, nor complicated ceremonial services.

The services were conducted with simplicity in the power and demonstration of the Holy Spirit. Paul told one church that he was very concerned about them because they were getting away from the simplicity of Christianity..."

As mentioned in our previous conversation on this subject, and I will say it again here for the abundance of clarity: "A Bishop may be the Senior Pastor of a local church, or the apostolic-Prophet or the prophetic-Apostle over several ministers and churches.

It is not necessarily a fivefold calling, but an administrative office that is given by others and not by oneself. I am scripturally convinced that the use of the title 'Bishop' is not wrong if the person bearing the title meets its qualifications and if the motive and purpose for its usage are according to Biblical principles. **But if the office of Bishop develops into a pyramid papal system as it did during the deterioration of the Church, then it becomes wrong."**

The Anointing Identifies - Not Religious Apparel
(That's Old Testament thinking!)

Ultimately, we are recognised by the anointing *(that makes way for us)* and not influence that's natural or gained by the arm of the flesh.

*Then he answered and spake unto me, saying, This is the word of the Lord unto Zerubbabel, saying, **Not by might, nor by power, but by my spirit, saith the Lord of hosts.***

(Zechariah 4:6 KJV)

Jesus refused to take on the natural title of a king, and denied all natural influence, in order to reveal His Father's influence and His Father's Kingdom. This too, and this alone, is the role of every minister of the gospel.

We are also not given to the same racist diatribe as the world around us; we are in it but not of it. The endless propaganda is just background noise. Jesus was a Jew! We are neither racist nor religious, and once again, in Christ we are bigger than that.

Amen!

Remember, if His Anointing is not manifest through your life and ministry, then perhaps you have faded into the background noise!

Dr Alan

ENDNOTES:

1. "Sexual Madness" by Drs Alan and Jenny Pateman, pages 55-57, Copyright © 2012, Second print/update 2020, Published by APMI Publications

2. Excerpts taken from "Apostles Prophets and the Coming Moves of God" God's End-Time Plans for His Church and Planet Earth, by Dr Bill Hamon, pages 173-178, Copyright © 1997, Published by Destiny Image Publishers, Inc. USA

3. This "Truth for the Journey" has been taken from: https://watchersofthe4kings.com

4. Scripture references marked ERV are taken from the Holy Bible: Easy-to-Read Version (ERV), International Edition © 2013, 2016 by Bible League International and used by permission.

5. Scripture references marked KJV are taken from the King James Version of the Bible.

6. Scripture quotations marked MSG are taken from The Message. Copyright © 1993, 1994, 1995, 1996, 2000, 2001, 2002. Used by permission of NavPress Publishing Group.

6❖

Ecumenical Movement

Truth for the Journey,
8th June 2018 – Watchers Letter

New Days – New Ways

They dress the wound of my people as though it were not serious. "Peace, peace," they say, when there is no peace *(Jeremiah 6:14).*

Welcome to another Truth for the Journey! Today we will cover an interesting topic, especially considering current events, involving such figureheads as the Pope and the Catholic Church. Throughout this letter, I have mentioned the Catholic Church numerous times, but within a specific context!

Before we begin let me clarify that currently my wife and I are living in Tuscany Italy, where I have had the opportunity to preach more than once in the Catholic Church. I have always found it to be "open" *(that is with the Charismatic Catholics)*, and in some cases "more-open-and-hungry" for the things of God than other churches I experience!

For instance, on several occasions I have preached for Padre Don Stefano, *(a charismatic Catholic priest)* who lives on top of a mountain here in Tuscany - and have enjoyed some spectacular events with him *(a mountain that takes roughly one and half hours to ascend - even with a car!)* The precise reason that he was placed there was due to his sincere belief in the things of the Holy Spirit.

Something that his peers in the Catholic Church did not collectively appreciate some decades before and decidedly "put-him-out-to-graze" in order to minimize the influence of his beliefs on others! In other words he was effectively "ostracized" by his own church in an attempt to quench the Holy Spirit's fire!

However as it says in John 12:32, if Jesus is lifted up, all men will be drawn to Him; therefore we know and have confidence that the Holy Spirit will always find a way to draw people unto Christ. Despite all their efforts, those in the hierarchy in the Catholic Church were unable to hinder the moving of the Holy Spirit for long, as Padre Don Stefano regularly attracts hundreds upon hundreds to his meetings on the mountain top.

Many came via the coach load *(totally disregarding the difficulty of logistics!)* especially for such calendar events as

"Pentecost." Where typically Don Stefano would invite known "Pentecostals" to come and preach for him on those specific occasions - which is where I came in of course!

So as you can tell, I have always and will always preach where the doors are open and where I feel the leading of God's Spirit, whom over the years I have discovered, will transcend any humanistic and religious boundary and anoint to preach right across the board; with strong love without ever compromising the scriptures.

So having said all this - by way of small disclaimer - nothing changes the fact that there are obvious discrepancies within the doctrine of the Catholic Church! Yet with nothing posing too great of a challenge or a threat for the Holy Spirit - keeping this in mind - let us read on, from this excerpt taken from my own book material on the End Times - entitled, "Israel, the Church and the End Times."[1]

The Coming Marriage of all Religions

It was interesting that several years ago, Archbishop Runcie who was the head of the Church of England, told "Time Magazine" that he had given a ring to Pope John Paul II as "an engagement ring" in view of the coming marriage between the Roman Catholic Church and the Church of England.

Remember the Church of Rome has not renounced any of the fundamental doctrinal errors that provoked the Protestant Reformation in AD1520. The non-Catholic members of the union are making this Ecumenical union on the basis of theological compromise.

If we are going to be swept up in the more recent events that have helped encourage a new wind of *ecumenical-fever,* we must first remember that unity comes via the Spirit and not man-made-structures. Let it also be said, that if it is the Spirit who unites us, already we are one! But if we depend on man-made-structures to unite us, then there can never be unity, *(the Babylonian structure will never sync with God's Spirit).*

In addition to this, Jesus never promised "religious-unity." Quite the opposite in fact! His choice of words in Matthew 10:34 were quite emphatic: *"Do not suppose that I have come to bring peace to the earth. I did not come to bring peace, but a sword."*

Catholic Theologians

Even Catholic theologians admit that John Paul II was the most traditional Pope of this last century and the strongest advocate of worship of Mary, Queen of Heaven, and Mother of God, as the "co-redemptrix" along with Jesus Christ. However a process of intense ecumenical dialogue has proceeded quietly during the last twenty years or so. The Church leaders are very close to healing the schism between the Greek and Russian Orthodox Churches and the Church of Rome.

The Pope met with Buddhist, Muslim, and Jewish religious leaders from around the world.

For the first time in history the Vatican has sought to establish ties with those other churches. He has engaged in ecumenical religious rituals and services with other religions that would have been unimaginable for any previous Pope.

Unity Based on Compromise

The danger today is that in opting for a man-made unity based on compromise and abandoning the Protestant Reformation and the truths of the scriptures that were sealed in the blood of martyrs, we are heading back to whence we came.

Michael de Semlyen says, today in Britain, there is a "love Gospel" about, which confines itself exclusively to what is called "the positive." It is claimed that as long as Jesus Christ is proclaimed as Saviour and Lord, we are all as one in Him. Differences over doctrine must not be allowed to get in the way of this. They say, **"we can affirm truth, but not confront error!"**

Even Evangelical Alliance, UK Director *(at the time),* Clive Calver said: "More barriers need to come down if a true alliance of evangelicals in the UK is to emerge. There are thousands more with whom we wish to stand shoulder to shoulder." Is this part of the New World Order? It must be said that those who are pointing the finger and accusing many who are standing for truth as sects, are very often part of the so-called "unity at any cost," which is part of the Babylonian church.

A. W. Tozer said, "Every century needs its prophetic voices. Those men who have been gifted by God with an incisive cutting edge to expose hypocrisy, denounce compromise, and call for holiness."

He said, "If THE CHURCH in the second half of this century is to recover from the injuries which she suffered in the first half, there must appear a new type of preacher. The proper ruler of the synagogue type will never do. Neither will the priestly type of man who carries out his duties, takes his pay and asks no questions, nor the smooth talking pastoral type who knows how to make the Christian religion acceptable to everyone.

All these have been tried and found wanting. Another kind of religious leader must arise among us. He must be of the old Prophet type, a man who has seen visions of God and has heard a voice from the throne.

The Protestant Martyrs

The Protestant Martyrs, godly and loving men, could have taken this same position of, peace at any cost, within the wider Church of their day. They could have confined themselves to avoiding all controversy and to agreeing with their persecutors about many of the 'positives.' But, the scripture commanded them to 'exhort and convince by sound doctrine' and to 'flee from idolatry.'

They obeyed; they saw the error and the idolatry, and as responsible leaders, as Pastors trusted to guide their flocks into green pastures, they exposed and opposed it all roundly. They could so easily have chosen to look the other way and concentrate on the many truths of the Christian faith, which was common ground. They could have elected to please men, rather than please God."

The Reformers however saw the whole Catholic system as anti-Christian. Luther and Calvin went so far as to identify the Papacy with the Antichrist and they like Wycliffe, Tyndale, Matthew Henry, Spurgeon, Llyod-Jones and many others saw the Roman Catholic Institution as Mystery Babylon, the Mother of Harlots, vividly described in Revelation 17.

The Spirit filled life is filled with testimony of experience, which of course is not wrong in itself, but "New Days, New Ways" is a dangerous way of life!

I well knew how many smooth arguments can be marshalled in support of the new cross.

-- A.W. Tozer

Does not the new cross win converts and make many followers and so carry the advantage of numerical success? Should we not adjust ourselves to the changing times? Have we not heard the slogan, *"New days, New ways"*? And who but someone very old and very conservative would insist upon death as the appointed way to life? And who today is interested in a gloomy mysticism that would sentence its flesh to a cross and recommend self-effacing humility as a virtue actually to be practised by modern Christians?

These are the arguments along with many more flippant still, which are brought forward to give an appearance of wisdom to the hollow and meaningless cross of popular Christianity.

Made Void the Cross

He says *(Tozer)*, "Doubtless there are many whose eyes are open to the tragedy of our times, but why are they so silent when their testimony is so sorely needed. In the name of Christ men have made void the cross of Christ. 'The noise of them that sing do I hear.' Men have fashioned a golden cross with a graving tool, and before it they sit down to eat and drink and rise up to play.

In their blindness they have substituted the work of their own hands for the working of God's power. Perhaps our greatest present need may be the coming of a Prophet to dash the stones at the foot of the mountain and call the Church out to repentance or to judgement...

Before all who wish to follow Christ the way lies clear. It is the way of death unto life. Always life stands just beyond death and beckons the man who is sick of himself to come and know the life more abundant. But to reach the new life he must pass through the valley of the shadow of death, and I know that at the sound of those words many will turn back and follow Christ no more. *But to whom shall we go? 'Thou hast the words of eternal life.'"*

To close, let us be mindful of all that has been brought out in this letter here, and resist becoming part of a false "Doctrine," whether Catholic, Anglican, Protestant or Pentecostal that cries "peace" when there is no peace! *(Jeremiah 6:14)* For those of us who entered into the life of Christ, we chose to be identified as such; an identity that we cannot afford to compromise.

In fact we live in a day where the distinctions are becoming more and more acute - in the context that the dark is getting darker and the brightness is getting brighter! In other words the dividing lines, although fudged for many are still strong. We must make our daily choices wisely and never lean back into deception.

Let us therefore not be fearful of hearing the voice of God's Prophets. Satan has undermined the authority of the "Prophet" in every generation, including this one - simply because they threaten him the most! Remember that God Himself singles them out when He declares, "Come not against Mine anointed ones, and against My prophets do not evil" *(1 Chronicles 16:22 YLT).*

They will always be "singled-out" so we must not be timid about them. Instead let us become a generation that develops "ears to hear" the voice of His Prophets - resisting our human instinct that "despises" this gift. They may not be as "smooth-talking" as the other gifts *(even much less articulate perhaps)* especially to the humanistic or woke crowd; but oh how we need this potent gift *(the Prophet)* in the Body of Christ today!

Amen.

He is Lord,
Dr Alan

PRAYER FOR THE DAY

Father I want to promote the one and only, true cross of Christ. Help me not fall into the trap of humanism, which cleverly marshals smooth arguments in support of a "new cross." Help me Father to live a life worthy of Christ and His Spirit, because without Him I know that I am nothing. Help me not to soak up or side with the "political correctness" of this generation, which has all but "invaded" Your Church. Help me "fail" to compromise when forced to choose between that and Your Word! Help me make the right choices in everything - "Christ and Christ alone" - whether in word or in deed. In Jesus' Name.

CONFESSION OF THE DAY

You are Life. You are my Source and Supply. You are Truth. Nothing that is said "outside" of You can be considered truth at all. You are my Rock and my Deliverer; my Redeemer. I AM REDEEMED. I think as one redeemed. I live as one redeemed. I communicate with the world around me as one who has been redeemed. I don't hide my redemption. I uphold neither a "false cross" nor a mixture of "humanistic arguments" but truth itself - Jesus Christ - who will draw all men unto Himself. I am not given to humanistic arguments, logic or reason - outside of Your Word. You are light. You are the Way. I follow You with my understanding, I follow with my heart. I follow with my whole spirit, soul and body. You alone are worthy. Hallelujah!

ENDNOTES:

1. "Israel, the Church and the End Times" by Dr Alan Pateman, Copyright © 2018, Published by APMI Publications

2. This "Truth for the Journey" has been taken from: https://watchersofthe4kings.com

3. Scripture quotations marked YLT are taken from the Young's Literal Translation of the bible.

7❖

The Harlot Church

Truth for the Journey
27th May 2014 – Watchers Letter

Mystery, Babylon the Great

In this Truth for the Journey today, we will further discuss the role that the Church and religion as a whole will play and the influence it will have on the world stage, during the culmination of this age.

Not everyone is clear on how things will play out. Scripture is vague in some areas and specific in others. Nevertheless there is a great "unfolding" occurring and only the **spiritually** discerning *(not elite nor exclusive)* will have any true perception about what's really going on *(Ephesians 1:17-19)*.

For instance some have thought that the Roman Catholic Church is the harlot church where the Antichrist will rule, and the city of Babylon being Rome, Italy. However the Harlot is not any *single* denominational structure. **She is an** *amalgamation* **of all the world's ecclesiastical, man-made religions,** *including* the present day denominations choosing to have only a *form* of godliness *(2 Timothy 3:5).*

Today the ancient harlot is about to receive a new vehicle through which she can function. Quite possibly it is the World Council of Churches, which works for the unity of all religions. While man-made religions are working to bring all Christians under their control, the Holy Spirit is working to bring them *(Christians)* together as the Glorious Church!

It is also possible that the city destroyed during mid-Tribulation will be the headquarters of the harlot religious system, or as some have identified it, the World Church. But its exact identity is unknown. Presently Geneva, Switzerland, is the headquarters of the World Council of Churches, World Bank centre, and is the city of treaties between nations.

As I mentioned in a previous letter, Grant R. Jeffrey, also mentions in his book **"Prince of Darkness"** that, "In a fascinating revelation, Archbishop Runcie of the Church of England told Time Magazine *(October 16, 1989)* that he had given a special ring to the Roman Pontiff. He explained that this ring was *'an engagement ring'* between him and Pope John Paul II as a promise of the coming union between the Church of England and the Church of Rome."

Grant Jeffrey goes on to expand this theme further by adding, "These ecumenical groups have often complained that the only real obstacle to their religious union was the resistance of the *evangelical conservative Christians*. Once these Christians are <u>removed</u> supernaturally by the Rapture, there most probably will be little resistance from any other group to its proposed union.

Ultimately this false world religion will involve an alliance of the Roman Catholic Church, the Russian and Greek Orthodox Churches, various Protestant groups, and New Age cult groups. **Virtually all religiously minded people will enthusiastically join this false church in a tremendous alliance with the new political leader of the New World Order, the Antichrist."**[1] *(It's clear then, that the Evangelical Alliance must also avoid falling into this trap!)*

Mother of Harlots

The Prophet John saw this future, satanically inspired alliance of religion and politics, as symbolised by the Babylon *"Mother of Harlots."* As John prophetically looked down the centuries he saw this world wide religious system supporting the Antichrist and the ten nations of his kingdom in their rise to power:

I saw a woman sitting upon a scarlet beast, which was full of names of blasphemy, having seven heads and ten horns. The woman was arrayed in purple and scarlet, and adorned with gold and precious stones having in her hand a golden cup full of abominations and filthiness of her fornication. And on her forehead a name was written:

MYSTERY, BABYLON THE GREAT, THE MOTHER OF HARLOTS AND ABOMINATIONS OF THE EARTH.

(Revelation 17:3-5 NKJV)

Apostasy and Blasphemy

Note that John saw the end-time false religious system *"sitting upon a scarlet beast."* This indicates that the religious system will initially be lifted up and honoured by the Antichrist's *political allies.* However, John reveals that this **last day religious system will be characterised by apostasy and blasphemy.** She will be known for her vast riches, yet her true secret nature is indicated by the Prophet's words, *"abominations and filthiness of her fornication."*

The bible often uses the imagery of sexual unfaithfulness to signify spiritual apostasy. This false church will wallow in sensuality and will express the materialistic spirit of these last days. It will be known as *"Mystery, Babylon the Great"* because it will secretly embody the Babylonian religious mysteries that have characterised every man-made religion and cult since man's rebellion at the Tower of Babel.[2]

Thank you Lord, that you have opened our eyes.
Dr Alan

PRAYER FOR THE DAY

Glorious Father, I keep praying that You may give to me the Spirit of wisdom and revelation, so that I may know You and Your ways better. I pray that the eyes of my heart may be enlightened in order that I may know the hope to which You have called me, and the riches of the glorious inheritance in Your holy people, including Your incomparably great power for us who believe. Amen

CONFESSION OF THE DAY

I have the victory in Jesus' name. My adversary is under my feet. I am not moved by adverse circumstances. I have been made the righteousness of God in Christ. I dwell in God's Kingdom and have peace and joy in His Holy Spirit.

ENDNOTES:

1. "Prince of Darkness" by Grant R. Jeffrey, page 228, Copyright © 1994, Published by Frontier Research Publications, USA

2. "Israel, the Church and the End Times" by Dr Alan Pateman, pages 84-85, Copyright © 2018, Published by APMI Publications

3. This "Truth for the Journey" has been taken from: https://watchersofthe4kings.com

4. Scripture quotations marked NKJV are taken from the New King James Version®. Copyright © 1982 by Thomas Nelson, Inc. Used by permission. All rights reserved.

8 ❖

New Age Philosophy

Truth for the Journey
8th September 2017 – Watchers Letter

Array of Philosophy

L et's come back to Jesus and be Delivered of a New Age spirit and know what it really means to be Born Again.

It's true to say, in today's world, life is very hectic. Yet as believers we have a phenomenal array of technology, media and rich teachings at our disposal. There's no lack seemingly.

Different revelations can be emphasized on, such as grace or prosperity for example and we unintentionally make superstars out of our favourite Preachers, Leaders,

Bishops, Pastors and Teachers. This is fine to a degree; the bible does say to give honour where honour is due *(Romans 13:7)*. The concern arises when we start worshipping them rather than God.

Preserving Spiritual Equilibrium

In addition, when we emphasize on one revelation, *(at the exclusion of all else)*, we lose balance and become spiritually disorientated without even realizing it.

The fact is, that many churches are following New Age concepts without even knowing it and have become accustomed to using New Age philosophy and sophisticated terminology, rather than that which *lifts up* the Lord Jesus Christ and increases our relationship with Him.

Some churches purposely start out that way, while others evolve that way by osmosis. They slowly lose sight of the truth and blend with the culture to avoid social or emotional conflicts. Deception creeps in through lack of teaching and maturity from those who are in positions of responsibility, who forget that it's our job to, "...refute arguments and theories and reasonings and every proud and lofty thing that **sets itself up against the true knowledge of God...**" *(2 Corinthians 10:5 AMPC)*

> *Demolishing arguments and ideas, every high-and-mighty* **philosophy that <u>pits itself against the knowledge of the one true God</u>.** *We are taking prisoners of every thought, every emotion...*
>
> *(2 Corinthians 10:5 VOICE)*

*The tools of our trade aren't for... manipulation, but they are for **demolishing that entire massively corrupt culture.** We use our powerful God-tools for smashing warped philosophies, tearing down barriers <u>erected against the truth of God</u>, fitting every loose thought and emotion and impulse into the structure of life shaped by Christ. Our tools are ready at hand for clearing the ground of every obstruction and building lives of obedience into maturity.*

(2 Corinthians 10:3-6 MSG)

The Doctrine of Demons

The infiltration of the doctrine of demons is nothing new to the church: "The wisdom of this world should never be mistaken for heavenly wisdom; **it originates below in the earthly realms, with the demons**" *(James 3:15 VOICE)*; "This superficial wisdom is not such as comes down from above, but is earthly, unspiritual *(animal),* even devilish *(demoniacal)*" *(James 3:15 AMPC)*; "This wisdom descendeth not from above, but is earthly, sensual, devilish" *(KJVS)*.

Notice that this counterfeit and devilish knowledge, wisdom wants one thing only: **"...to set itself up against the knowledge of God."** And if it goes unchallenged, will indeed succeed in establishing itself as the acceptable *truth* of the culture. Embedded into society via the educational systems and social media for example.

My wife has recently written a book about this subject and one particular chapter she entitled, "Tolerance the god of this Age sits on the Throne of Culture" *(I recommend that you read it!)*

Don't lose Sight of the CROSS

However, I would suggest, that **LOSING SIGHT OF THE CROSS** is one of the biggest dangers that we face, especially as believers. Scripture clearly teaches that we must, "take up our crosses daily." Something that is done "daily" determines "lifestyle." Therefore taking up our crosses daily, points to a surrendered lifestyle.

> *Anyone who intends to come with me has to let me lead. You're not in the driver's seat---I am. Don't run from suffering; embrace it. Follow me and I'll show you how. Self-help is no help at all.*
>
> *Self-sacrifice is the way, my way, to finding yourself, your true self.* *What good would it do to get everything you want and lose you, the real you? If any of you is embarrassed with me and the way I'm leading you, know that the Son of Man will be far more embarrassed with you when he arrives in all his splendor in company with the Father and the holy angels.*
>
> (Luke 9:23-27 MSG)

See just how counter cultural this is? **"Self help is no help at all."** Try telling that to this narcissistic generation, who are totally surrendered to their emotions and feelings and any thought of "self denial" would be considered "abusive!" As believers, we are not swayed by the culture, we have God's Word to go on, not our feelings.

So let's just take a look to see where we may need to adjust our thinking and experience Christ anew with fresh revelation and infilling of His Holy Spirit, Amen.

See you in the next one!
Dr Alan

ENDNOTES:

1. This "Truth for the Journey" has been taken from: https://watchersofthe4kings.com

2. Scripture references marked AMPC are taken from the Amplified® Bible (AMPC), Copyright © 1954, 1958, 1962, 1964, 1965, 1987 by The Lockman Foundation. Used by permission. www.Lockman.org

3. Scripture references marked KJVS are taken from the Strong's Concordance with KJV. Taken from the TecartaBible App, © 2017 Tecarta, Inc. Version 7.11.5. Used by permission. All rights reserved.

4. Scripture quotations marked MSG are taken from The Message. Copyright © 1993, 1994, 1995, 1996, 2000, 2001, 2002. Used by permission of NavPress Publishing Group.

5. Scripture quotations marked VOICE are taken from The Voice™. Copyright © 2008 by Ecclesia Bible Society. Used by permission. All rights reserved.

9 ❖

New Age is in the Church

Truth for the Journey
10th September 2017 – Watchers Letter

What does The New Age Really Look Like?

It's rather hard to define or neatly package into one overarching concept or central theme. In fact it's very *nebulous,* meaning that it's so vast in its own concepts that it's purposely vague and ambiguous. It would take copious amounts of ink and paper to try and I'm not that willing to devote that much time to it in this letter!

However the basic premise is that man wants to achieve his own *state of headship and goodness,* one that he can control and determine. Just like running after the *things* of God without running after God Himself. Having a form of religion but denying the power of it. Even attempting to become greater or more prominent than Christ Himself.

Self-Deification

This leads me to *apotheosis* or *self-deification*. One psychologist recently wrote:

> *Self-deification is the perfect antidote for feeling inadequate. It's much simpler than learning or growing.* ***Don't improve; prove! Prove you're a god!***
> -- *Jeremy E Sherman Ph.D.*

Recently we had a paper submitted to our LICU University, by one of our students *(Rev Benjamin Noumba Mbock – Cameroon)* in Africa, about the growth of the Church, and the influence of the New Age in the African church. It's one of the best papers I've ever read from one of our students, from an African perspective. Which is important to me, as I've been called to work with the African church all over the world.

His paper concerned the genuine growth of the African church versus the influence of the New Age movement. Now not many associate the African church with the New Age movement, but as a mature minister, this particular student laid out his argument very well; it was a compelling read, which led to this particular letter.

One would associate witchcraft with Africa but not necessarily the New Age, which is more of a Western enterprise *(albeit the same thing - witchcraft)*, it's just branded differently. It's a bit more sophisticated and palatable for European gentry perhaps, than the local African village witch doctor!

He talked about the growth numbers in the African church not being authentic and that the New Age has infiltrated the African church, with many Pastors teaching New Age philosophy rather than scripture and revelation.

Philosophies are more acceptable than the Truth!

Those responsible in our churches, worldwide have a responsibility to teach God's Word, first and foremost. Whether it's from an African viewpoint or any other, the fact is that the whole world is being impacted by deception and **many Pastors are teaching New Age, self-help concepts, psychology and philosophy, because it's more** *acceptable* **to the general public.**

> *One of the biggest advantages we have as New Agers is once the occult, metaphysical, and New Age terminology is removed* **we have concepts and techniques that are very** <u>acceptable</u> **to the general public.**
>
> -- *Dick Stuphen*

Jesus and His message were always counter-cultural, from a secular point of view, but now also even within a growing church culture!

When we prefer the culture, to the Spirit of God, that's when we side with it. We can reach the culture without siding with it. Of course God wants to reach into secular culture and reach every generation but we must side with God and His truth every time, **"His truth endureth to *all* generations"** *(Psalm 100:5 KJVS)*. "Suppose ye that I am come to give peace on earth? I tell you, Nay; but rather division" *(Luke 12:51)*.

Yes! I am called to the African church. Every country I arrive in, I end up preaching to Africans. But it saddens me to see that others are not willing to cross-pollinate the same way. They remain colour-bound. I choose to remain colour-blind. I go where God tells me, because His Kingdom thrives on diversity. We should have Chinese, Spanish, Italian, American, African, British, German and Belgians etc., in our churches. That's Kingdom!

Leaders who are not called by God

There are many leading churches today, which are not even called by God to be in that position. They are too easily threatened and can't relate to other leaders outside of their ego-bubble. They start churches in pursuit of self-aggrandisement.

In Italy we have 100s of isolated little churches and I see Pastors continuing to struggle. In many cases they are supposedly *relating* to some Bishop or Apostle in Africa somewhere, but really they're just being *pimped* for money. It's fake piety and a religious brand of trafficking.

That's extreme! Yes it is. It's prostituting the church for profit: **"Perverse** disputings of men of corrupt minds, and destitute of the truth, **supposing that gain is godliness:** from such withdraw thyself. But godliness with contentment is great gain" *(1 Timothy 6:5-6)*.

I've seen men raised up into positions of leadership that they were never appointed by God to be in. They belong in the market place *(and vice versa)*. They bring out books and perform power-point messages in churches all over the world, but there's no *power* to any of it. They dress right, sound right, look right - but it's all wrong!

Lust is Rampant in the Church

I've gone to churches were *lust* is rife. Evidenced in the way that people dress. Look around, see the flirtatious and tight fitting clothes on both men and women, either too tight or cut too low. It's a secular social club mentality with a bit of church culture mixed in.

I've preached in churches where it was revealed to me that homosexuals were leading the worship and female prostitutes were members of the choir! This too was common knowledge to the Elders, who met regularly for *tricks* after church. Why is this happening? It's because there's no emphasis on holiness in these places. *We are talking about church people!*

Recently in a viral and passionate Facebook Live video, **Prophetess Juanita Bynum** called out all "scantily dressed female ministers," and told them to put some clothes on saying: *"How are you coming to church on a Sunday morning to worship God and you have no bra on?"* She had "so" much more to say, but she certainly has a point![1]

Many won't like what I'm saying here, but those with a true spirit will always applaud the truth. Always remember

God's yoke is easy, He is great, but the devil is always a liar. They are *not* equal opposites. There is no yin and yang.

God is mighty - Jesus Christ is Lord.

Dr Alan

ENDNOTES:

1. Watch! https://www.youtube.com/watch?v=oa2UPbcXbBc

2. This "Truth for the Journey" has been taken from: https://watchersofthe4kings.com

10 ❖

Unity and Reconciliation

Truth for the Journey
29th June 2018 – Watchers Letter

Denominational Structure

For it is by grace you have been saved, through faith—and this not from yourselves, it is the gift of God— not by works, so that no one can boast *(Ephesians 2:8-9)*.

Some years ago, Kenneth Copeland received a video from Pope Francis who asked for prayer and unity of the Spirit. Then the late Kim Clement prophesied about a new move of reconciliation around the world, declaring that Pope Francis has been handpicked by God to bring unity to the Body of Christ world-wide *(the word catholic means universal)*.

We need to take a moment to examine how we as Pentecostals, Charismatics, "Born Again believers" or Evangelicals etc., should respond to these declarations! As we all have limited understanding, limited by our own cultures, church experiences and denominational theology.

Personally I want to embrace all that God is doing throughout the world. One thing I have discovered is that God won't be boxed into anyone's traditions or preferences.

Reformation and Planned Reconciliation

After the Reformation many of the formerly Protestant churches were planning to reconcile with Rome and re-join the church our ancestors *"protested"* against. They *(our ancestors)* brought back the simple New Testament message of repentance and forgiveness; personal belief in Jesus and His once and for all sacrifice for sin on the cross, be all that is required for salvation.

They knew from scripture that all comes as a free gift from God, totally undeserved. "And being made perfect, he became the author of eternal salvation unto all them that obeyed him" *(Hebrews 5:9)*. They obeyed Him by believing the entire bible and **living and dying by it - and for it.**

In the book **"The Battle for World Evangelism,"** by Arthur Johnston, he says, "Emilio Núñez had the delicate and demanding task of spelling out the position Evangelicals should take toward the Roman Catholic Church in his paper entitled **'The Position of the Church Toward Aggiornamento'"** *(spirit of change and open-mindedness).*

Pre-Conciliar and Biblical Renewal

He claimed that this subject had been imposed on Evangelicals by the solo-religious realities resulting in the post-Vatican II conciliar church. A marked difference exists between the pre-conciliar church in liturgy and biblical renewal. Evangelicals could be most encouraged by the latter.

Of all the changes in *Post-Conciliar Catholicism* there is none more promising of better things in the lives of thousands of Catholics than that related to the new attitude of the Roman Church toward the Sacred Scriptures. We must confide in the redeeming power of the scriptural revelation.

Faith comes by hearing, and hearing by the word of God.
(Romans 10:17 NKJV)

He that believed that the renewal sought by John XXIII had become a revolution threatening the very foundations of traditional Catholicism.

Three well-defined tendencies have developed in contemporary Catholicism:

- **First** traditionalism that closes the door to any fundamental change in doctrine.

- **Second** progressivism with its concern to reinterpret Catholic doctrine and effect a basis transformation in the structure of the church.

- **Third** moderate Catholicism in the style of John XXIII, who wanted to renew the church within the context of traditional theology.

This inner struggle for self-renewal is further complicated for Latin American Evangelicals by the unexpected hand of ecumenical friendship extended by the Catholics to the Protestants. Evangelical churches cannot, Núñez said, remain indifferent to this extended hand.

Núñez then entered into the inter-evangelical debate that begins with the confusion created in the mind of one that is converted from Catholicism to Protestantism. It is natural to ask, **"If the Roman Catholic Church is our sister, why was I invited to leave it to embrace Protestantism?"**

Closer Relations with Rome!

Some Protestants favour closer relations with Rome; many others do not! Let's begin to examine the call to Protestants, for unity by the late Bishop Tony Palmer and Pope Francis at the Kenneth Copeland Ministries Ministerial Conference.

The question is this, was the late Tony Palmer calling all denominations to be reconciled to God, or was he calling all Protestants to be reconciled to the Catholic Church? He goes on to say, "If you are Born Again you are Catholic because," he says, "the word Catholic does not mean Roman, it means universal." He then says to take back what belongs to us, which is to be Catholic!

But in the book of Acts chapter 11:26, we are told that the church in Antioch were first called Christians *(not Catholic)*, even the church at Rome.

The name "Christian" bound the believers together, though they were in many self-autonomous churches. The name "Catholic" came about through centralization of the churches *(not all)*, into a denomination. It is clear to me that denominations do not inherit the Kingdom of God.

A False Gospel

In fact it's true to say, that it's only in the last 20 years since "The Joint Declaration on the Doctrine of Justification"- JDDJ *(1999)*, that the Catholic church has excepted and made a declaration along with the Lutherans, that salvation is by Grace and not works. I dare say that if that is true, then the Catholic Church has been preaching a false gospel for hundreds of years!

Those who favour the ecumenical encounter say... that the Holy Spirit is moving in an unusual way in the Roman Catholic Church, and that the Evangelicals should be very careful in their anti-ecumenism, or they may be opposing the Work of God. The other group asks if it is possible that the Spirit should approve an ecclesiastical relation that can compromise certain truths that He Himself has inspired. Besides they say, if the Spirit has begun an extraordinary work among the Catholics, is it not certain that an anti-Biblical ecumenism would hinder it rather than help it?

Supporters of the ecumenical dialogue affirm that opposition to it demonstrates a serious lack of love toward Catholics. Opponents say that out of love for Catholics they desire to preserve the integrity of the Gospel - and who has demonstrated more love *(for in the scripture love is not divorced from the truth)* than those who have given their lives as pioneers or martyrs?

Catholic-Protestant Ecumenism

Another argument in favour of Catholic-Protestant ecumenism is the affirmation that the Perfect Church doesn't exist on the face of the earth. The reply to this argument is that although it is conceded that there is no perfect ecclesiastical community, this doesn't oblige anyone to unite with a Church whose errors are evident in the light of the bible.

Evangelical uncertainties about the future of Catholicism should not pressure them into rejecting it, some say, for it is not known what is going on inside. Others disagree with the principle of *"waiting,"* because there are norms in God's Word ***"that guide the Church along paths of right doctrine and morals, or must she depend only on the march of human events to determine her way?"*** The path of evangelical relativism, Núñez fears, and "the parenthesis of waiting may send many souls into an eternity without God, without Christ, and without hope..."

The word "Aggiornamento" *(that means, "a bringing up to date," which was used to mean a **"spirit of change and open-mindedness"** during the Second Vatican Council - otherwise known as "Vatican II" - in 1959),* should not lead to an unfounded optimism that minimises the post-conciliar differences and maximises the similarities, for aggioraments has not ushered in any fundamental changes in questions of: tradition, authority of scriptures, papal infallibility, synergism, sacramentalism, mariology, purgatory, and prayers for the dead.

This also includes praying to Saints for miracles, then stigmata, such as in the case of the late Padre Pio, of Pietrelcina, who is famous amongst the Catholics here in Italy.

Our confessions are considered incomplete, and Roman Catholicism in *"the Church par excellence"* for *"the ecclesia semper reformanda* is also the *ecclesia semper eadem."* Núñez agreed with Francis Schaeffer's belief that Roman Catholicism was moving more and more toward a humanism that would make a relationship with ecumenical Protestantism more compatible.

The latter affirms that it is *"not necessary or even correct to evangelise Catholics"* because *"they are already incorporated into the redeemed community as a result of their baptism in the Catholic Church..."*

Clear Denunciation of Error

The Evangelical must be positive in his teaching and practice but **"relevant proclamation of the Christian Message includes also the clear and conclusive denunciation of error, where ever this threatens the life of the Church that Christ bought with His blood."**

Individual friendships with Roman Catholics are to be encouraged but Ecumenical dialogue was discouraged.

In reality, to maintain burning in our hearts the flame of evangelistic zeal is one of the best antidotes against any theological or ecclesiastical movement that threatens the Church with paralysis in her missionary function.

Our Own Evangelical Heritage

The official translation of the final *"Evangelical Declaration of Bogota"* (1969) decided by a vote of the Congress that:

In a continent where the majority is nominal Catholics, we cannot shut our eyes to the ferment of renewal within the Church of Rome. The *"aggiornamento"* faces us up both with risk and opportunity: change in liturgy, ecclesiology, politics and strategy still have untouched the dogmas, which separate evangelicals from Rome.

Nevertheless, our trust in the Word of God, the distribution and reading of which continue to accelerate within Catholicism, value use to hope for fruit of renewal, and they present us with an opportunity for dialogue on a personal level.

This needs to be an intelligent dialogue, and it demands from our churches a deeper and more consistent teaching of our own evangelical heritage, so as to avoid the risks of a false and misunderstood ecumenism.

Hope all of this is helpful,
Dr Alan

PRAYER FOR THE DAY

Heavenly Father, I thank You that You lead me into all truth, by Your Word and Spirit. Thank You for the gift of wisdom, love and grace, Amen.

CONFESSION OF THE DAY

Jesus is Lord over my spirit, my soul, and my body. He has been made unto me wisdom, righteousness, sanctification and redemption. I am a member of the Body of Christ here on earth. I honour Him and live to bring glory to His name. To which every knee shall bow and every tongue confess that He is Lord! Scripture declares I have the mind of Christ; therefore I can have His mind on every issue, especially His thoughts, feelings and purposes towards His own Body.

ENDNOTES:

1. This "Truth for the Journey" has been taken from: https://watchersofthe4kings.com

2. Scripture quotations marked NKJV are taken from the New King James Version®. Copyright © 1982 by Thomas Nelson, Inc. Used by permission. All rights reserved.

11 ❖

The Way of the Church

Truth for the Journey
9th June 2017 – Apostolic Clarification

Apostles and Prophets

From personal experience when I travel throughout Europe, it's easier to use the word Apostle than Bishop. Yet when in African churches, there is a much greater emphasis on Bishops and Archbishops, who are held in great esteem, while all others gifts or offices are perceived as being beneath such hierarchy.

Dr Bill Hamon says, "Religious people have a way of taking what is scriptural, sacred and workable and converting it into a lifeless religious form and a pyramid hierarchal structure that restricts God's purpose and brings bondage to His people. When the church becomes more structural than spiritual, it becomes petrified wood instead of a fruitful growing tree with the sap flowing.

When it becomes more spiritual than structural, it becomes like dissipating and destructive floodwaters without any control or order. For this reason, both Apostles and Prophets must be prominent and coequal in laying the foundation for the church. No church will have a balance and proper foundation and function without the ministry of both Apostles and Prophets."[1]

I'm not saying we should now throw the baby out with the bathwater and get rid of all the Bishops. Not at all! Though correct and balanced teaching *must* be brought back into the church, especially where leadership positions and titles are concerned.

Bishop a Congregational Elder

There is nothing in this system, which corresponds exactly to the modern diocese episcopate, Bishops, when they are mentioned *(Philippians 1:1)* are from a board of local congregational officers and the position occupied by Timothy and Titus is that of Paul's personal lieutenants in his missionary work. It seems most likely that he was then specially designated with the title of Bishop; but even when the monarchical Bishop appears in the letters of Ignatius, he is still the Pastor of a single congregation.

As we have already seen at the beginning of this book, the word **episkopos** occurs five times in the NT: once of Christ

(1 Peter 2:25) and in four places of "Bishops" or **"Overseers"**
in local churches *(Acts 20:28; Philippians 1:1; 1 Timothy 3:2;
Titus 1:7)*. The verb **episkopeo** occurs in Hebrews 12:15
("watching") and *(in some NT MSS)* 1 Peter 5:2 *("exercising the
oversight")*.

A Bishop then has "oversight of," he is an "Overseer."
1 Peter 5:2 says, "Feed the flock of God which is among
you, taking the oversight thereof" *(KJV)*. The Greek word
for "oversight" is **episkopeo,** Strong's #1983 - to oversee, to
beware, to look diligently, takes the oversight. Extra words
given: direction *(about the times)*, have charge of, take aim at
(spy), regard, consider, take heed, look at *(on)*, mark.

Clearly Misunderstood

Recently on a ministry trip to South Africa, I was asked
to be involved in a presbytery, during a particular ordination
service. Some of those individuals to be ordained that day, I
might add, were accomplished men and women in their own
right. One in particular was acting chaplain to a very high-
ranking government official within his own country and was
held in very high regard.

However during the process of this extremely
ceremonial meeting, they proceeded to make such a fan fare
of these prospective Bishops, to the point that it was almost
ridiculous! The last person they ordained that day was a
woman Evangelist, whom they ordained an Apostle and
whom they gave very little prominence to at all. They clearly
misunderstood the *governing role* and *office* of an Apostle,
versus the general *overseeing role* of a Bishop.

"The **word Bishop is found four times** in the King James New Testament, **the word APOSTLE is found over seventy times.** You do the math. Which ministry is emphasized more by the Holy Spirit? In addition to these numbers the term 'Bishop' has had a history of misuse. It has presently come to mean something that it never meant in the early church. Because of this the church has suffered in its understanding of apostolic ministry. This is unfortunate because the Apostle's ministry is much needed today."[2]

Bishops Must Relate to an Apostle!

However we cannot allow confusion to reign unchallenged in the Body of Christ, especially concerning such important matters as these and thus fuels my passion even more, to help restore some clarity back into the church, about the true position, nature and role of the Apostle; in regards to the other five-fold-ministry gifts, as well as putting the record straight about Bishops who were originally and basically commissioned as *overseers* for the local church.

Only by turning to scripture can we reveal the true position-that-goes-with-the-title and show up whether or not certain *replacement doctrine* has crept into the church. Once error is embraced, it readily circulates throughout the rest of the body like a virus that must be stopped and corrected.

Consider Paul in whose writings he often declared himself, "Paul an Apostle." Why? Because Paul knew exactly who he was and what he was commissioned to do. This should be true of the rest of us, because there is clear foundation and structure to the Body of Christ, which Jesus Himself put into place.

By the grace God has given me, I laid a foundation as an expert builder, and someone else is building on it. But each one should be careful how he builds...

(1 Corinthians 3:10)

He is more than just an architect; He is like a "superintendent" of the building process. *Strong's #5045 tekton (tek'-tone); from the base of 5098: an artificer (as producer of fabrics), i.e. (specially) a* **craftsman** *in wood: KJV - carpenter.*

This apostolic function is the necessary basis for every local church, which forms part of the household of God. "Consequently, you are no longer foreigners and aliens, but fellow citizens with God's people and members of God's household, built on the foundations of the Apostles and Prophets, with Christ Jesus Himself as the chief cornerstone" *(Ephesians 2:19-20).*[3]

See you in the next one!
Dr Alan

ENDNOTES:

1. "Apostles, Prophets and the Coming Moves of God" by Dr Bill Hamon, page 147, Copyright © 1997, Published by Destiny Image Publishers, Inc. USA

2. Online article: "Apostles or Bishops?" by John Eckhardt, John Eckhardt Ministries, www.johneckhardtministries.com

3. "Apostles, Can the Church Survive Without Them?" by Dr Alan Pateman, pages 23-26. Copyright © 2012, Published by APMI Publications

4. This "Truth for the Journey" has been taken from: https://watchersofthe4kings.com

5. Scripture references marked KJV are taken from the King James Version of the Bible.

12❖

Reformation and Restoration

Truth for the Journey
15th June 2018 – Apostolic Restoration

For the Development of the Saints

Your **Kingdom come, Your will be done on earth as it is in heaven!** *(Matthew 6:10)*

Welcome to this Truth for the Journey! I know you will enjoy taking this journey with me, as I use this particular letter on the "Apostolic Reformation," to help bring much needed teaching and clarity to the Church.

I want to address the fact that we are currently living in the time of the Apostolic Reformation, where the apostolic ministry is the last of the fivefold ministries to be fully restored to the Body of Christ before He can return *(and I will explain in full).*

However, like all genuine moves of God, the restoration of the apostolic is coming under some real and lasting fire, from some pretty aggressive political and religious quarters. Nevertheless it continues to accelerate as one of the fastest growing moves of God happening on this planet right now and the persecution only fans the flames higher, as it continues to spread with fervour.

This series of letters is therefore dedicated to all things surrounding the last apostolic reformation movements and all that they entail!

The Fivefold Ministry

This consists of the five offices and gifts mentioned in Ephesians 4:11: Apostles, Prophets, Evangelists, Pastors and Teachers, bringing unity and maturity to the Body of Christ.

> *So Christ himself gave the apostles, the prophets, the evangelists, the pastors and teachers, to equip his people for works of service, so that the body of Christ may be built up until we all reach unity in the faith and in the knowledge of the Son of God and become mature, attaining to the whole measure of the fullness of Christ.*
> *(Ephesians 4:11-13)*

Apostles are like fathers and mothers who impart to the Body of Christ and raise them up as sons and daughters in the faith. **Prophets** bring supernatural revelation and insight, giving vision of the times and seasons of God so that saints know what to do. **Teachers** teach the Word of God with simplicity and wisdom. **Pastors** nurture the Body of Christ with counselling, clothing them with Christ-like armour and garments. **Evangelists** impart zeal for souls to be saved and equip the saints with wisdom and anointing in winning the lost –Dr Bill Hamon.[1]

The Right Oversight

As stated before, religious people have a way of taking what is scriptural, sacred and workable and converting it into a **lifeless religious form and a pyramid hierarchal structure** that restricts God's purpose and brings bondage to His people. When the Church becomes more structural than spiritual, it becomes petrified wood instead of a fruitful growing tree with the sap flowing. When it becomes more spiritual than structural, it becomes like dissipating and destructive floodwaters **without any control or order.**

For this reason, both Apostles and Prophets must be prominent and coequal in laying the foundation for the Church. **No church will have a balanced and proper foundation and function without the ministry of both Apostles and Prophets.**[2]

Many wonderful life-giving miracles will be restored in the coming Apostolic Movement. The main thing will be the complete restoration of Apostles to their full recognition, acceptance, powerful ministry, place and position within the Body of Christ.

This new generation of Apostles will not be sterile hybrids that cannot reproduce like kind. They will have the Genesis principle declaring that every seed shall produce after its own kind. The restoration movement of the late 40's brought the revelation that there are still Prophets and Apostles in the Church. But they did not receive the revelation and anointing for reproducing other Apostles and Prophets.

Now the Apostolic Movement will bring the anointing for reproducing thousands of Apostles just as the Prophetic Movement reproduced thousands of Prophets...[3]

God's true Apostles will come forth, but there will arise false apostles, the immature, the wrongly motivated and the pseudo apostles who will bring reproach and make an improper, unbalanced presentation during the Apostolic Movement. And like all restoration movements, there will be those in the Apostolic Movement who will take some things to the extreme left and right...[4]

The Last-Day Ministry

When the Apostles are restored in their fullness, it will activate many things. It will cause many prophecies concerning the end times to start coming to pass at an accelerated rate. It is like a great machine that needs five things to happen in sequence before it will fully work.

It could be compared to a space rocket booster that must have five switches turned on before it can launch the space shuttle - the Church. Each switch or button represents one of the fivefold ministries.

The Evangelist switch was turned on fully in the 1950's and it made progressive preparation for the launching of the

Church space shuttle. The restoration of the **Pastor** in the 1960's to his proper role did the same things. It was the same with the restoration of the **Teacher** in the 1970's. The booster rockets turned on with all their fiery force in the 1980's with the restoration of the **Prophet** and God's great company of Prophets. With the full restoration of the **Apostle** and God's great company of Apostles, the space shuttle of the Church will be launched to fulfil its end-time ministry and eternal destiny.[5]

The Final restoration of Apostles will cause all ministers who will receive it to be raised to a higher level of anointing and ministry. It will revolutionize the whole function of the Church. It would be compared to how the world functioned at the beginning of the 20th century in travel, electronics and communication and how it functioned at the end of the century.[6]

Restoration movements that re-establish the ministries of the Prophets and Apostles in the Church are thriving as we speak, on unparalleled levels and we need to embrace all that God is doing in the earth today, as it ultimately ushers in the return of our Lord Jesus Christ.

This is Your Time,
Dr Alan

**APMI Motto: "Hearing His Voice
is all the Provision You Need"**

ENDNOTES:

1. http://www1.cbn.com/700club/dr-bill-hamon-restoring-fivefold-ministry

2. "Apostles, Prophets and the Coming Moves of God" by Dr Bill Hamon, page 175, Copyright © 1997, Published by Destiny Image Publishers, Inc. USA.

3. (Ibid P 211)

4. (Ibid P 212)

5. (Ibid P 221)

6. (Ibid P 222)

7. This "Truth for the Journey" has been taken from: https://watchersofthe4kings.com

13❖

Kingdom Identified

Truth for the Journey
16th October 2012 – His Kingdom

Creating a Perfect Society

Repent, for the kingdom of heaven is at hand *(Matthew 4:17)*.

Welcome to today's Truth for the Journey! Here we will continue with our discovery of His Kingdom and its true identity. Let's begin by saying that since the very beginning of history, men have always tried to create the "perfect" society!

For instance the famous Greek philosophers like Plato always dreamt of the "ideal society" - based upon ethical, political and social philosophies – but in reality their desires were always too "idealistic" ever to be realized!

When it comes to the bible however, it was first via the Old Testament Prophets that a picture of a future age emerged, where men would live together without armaments of war! *(This was something that Plato and others where idealistically "reaching" for but would never find "unattainable" based on their humanistic and philosophical ideals that were **outside of God!**)*

It was Isaiah who spoke of spears being turned into pruning hooks, and nations not lifting up swords against each other. In fact, the peace of the world would be so dramatically different that he used the images of a wolf lying down with a lamb, leopards with kids, and calves with young lions to signify the radical change in world affairs, which would come in the future.

Repentance is the Entry

As our opening scripture states, the message, which Jesus preached, was one of repentance because the beginning of a new era was at hand *(Matthew 4:17)* and His teachings, illustrations, and parables primarily dealt with the Kingdom of God. Including the prayer that He taught His disciples, *"Thy kingdom come, thy will be done on earth as it is in heaven"* *(Matthew 6:10)*. Jesus continually emphasised the Kingdom with His disciples.

When studying the gospels this is very plain to see but when it comes to Matthew's gospel he called it the "Kingdom of heaven" simply because it was written primarily for the Jews. However it remains that little agreement exists on what the Kingdom of God is and what the message of the gospel of the Kingdom should be.

Dr Paul Y. Cho in his book, "More Than Numbers" states, "Augustine perceived the Kingdom of God to be synonymous with the church. The Reformed movement had a large part in redefining the meaning of the Kingdom of God. Calvin basically agreed with Augustine. He differed on what aspect of the church represented the Kingdom of God. His feelings were that the true church, which was within the obvious church, was the earthly manifestations of the Kingdom of God.

The Task of the Church

The task of the church would be made possible by the use of a special power called the gospel of the Kingdom of God. **This gospel of the Kingdom of God would so affect the lives of first men and then nations that there would be a mighty transformation of social, political, and economic reality.** The church was likened to leaven which would slowly so permeate the dough of the earth that at a point in history the earth would proclaim Jesus Christ as Lord and King.

At this point the Lord Jesus Christ would return to earth to accept the Kingdom prepared for Him by his heavenly Father.

There has been another school of theology, which does not try to explain the Kingdom of God in terms of the future but tries to understand the Kingdom of God in its present social context. *Harvey Cox* is just one of many modern theologians who view the Kingdom of God as a social order brought about by the church.

The problems of inequality, prejudice, as well as the rest of our social concerns are to be addressed and dealt with by a church, which is conscious of its mission. Biblical terms are redefined to make them more relevant of today's problems. Many of our liberal church leaders are motivated by what they see as the lack of concern, within the more conservative evangelical church leaders."[1]

However theological views of the Kingdom of God are intrinsically flawed and a much greater foundation exists than mere "reason" for establishing what the Kingdom of God really is, which is the very Word of God.

The following are basic biblical principles that reveal what the Kingdom of God is:

1. Future and Present:

The Kingdom of God is not only for the future, but also for the present. *"For the kingdom of God is not meat and drink; but righteousness, and peace, and joy in the Holy Ghost" (Romans 14:17).* Paul reveals to us that the Kingdom of God transcends the natural existence of man and caused him to experience in the here and now, the fruit of the Holy Spirit. That if you associate with the Holy Spirit you will become like the person you are associating with.

The natural result of association with the Holy Spirit will be a way of life, which is more concerned with the quality God bestows to life rather than the essential aspects to life, eating and drinking.

2. To Change Sides:

Paul also reveals that the Kingdom of God is something that we have entered into as a result of our being regenerated by the Holy Spirit. *"[God] hath delivered us from the power of darkness, and hath translated us into the kingdom of his dear Son" (Colossians 1:13).* The word, "translated," used in our English text, in the Greek is ***metestasen,*** which literally means to change sides.

As I study this verse, I see a picture of a football game. Each team is on the opposite end of the field. On one side is the team, which represents the kingdom of darkness. On the other side is the team, which represents the Kingdom of God. During the game, one of the main players of the darkness team takes off his shirt and number, goes to the opposing bench and puts on the Kingdom of God shirt. Then he goes on the field to play against the darkness boys. He simply switches sides. This is what happened to us. We were transformed from one kingdom to the other, the Kingdom of our Lord.

3. Eternal Blessedness:

The Kingdom of God is also described in its future prospect for eternal blessedness. *"Wherefore the rather, brethren, give diligence to make your calling and election sure: for if ye do these things, ye shall never fall: For so an entrance shall be ministered unto you abundantly in the everlasting kingdom of our Lord and Saviour Jesus Christ" (2 Peter 1:10-11 KJV).*

In Matthew Jesus spoke of the future when he said, *"Many will come from the east and west and sit at the table with*

Abraham, Isaac and Jacob in the kingdom of heaven" (8:11). Yet in Matthew 13, our Lord tells parables which give further clarification to what He meant by the Kingdom of heaven. He says that once the Kingdom is purged, the righteous would shine like the sun.

4. True Representation:

Jesus is the representation of what it is like to be in the Kingdom. *"The kingdom of God is not coming with signs to be observed; nor will they say, 'Lo, here it is!' or 'There!' for behold, the kingdom of God is in the midst of you"* (Luke 17:20-21 RSV). This verse can be applied to the fact that the Kingdom of God was there in their midst. The "you" here is the plural, which in English is hard to understand. Jesus was there in their midst. The Pharisees were not to look for a glorious manifestation in the future, but the Kingdom was before them and they were too blind to observe that God was working without a lot of fanfare.

5. Balanced Understanding:

The Kingdom's paradox has to be viewed on the basis of a balanced understanding. Jesus told Pilate in John 18, *"My kingdom is not of this world."* Yet He also said in Luke 13 that the Kingdom of God would start out rather unobservable, like a mustard seed. Yet, this seed, almost unnoticed, would grow up and affect the entire world.

Rather than seeing opposing views in scripture as contradictory, I consider them as a balance. Therefore, the Kingdom of God is future, but it is present. It is not of this world, but it affects this world. It can be entered into at the present time, but there is a future fulfilment. You can't see it with the natural eye, but the Kingdom of God is everywhere Christ is. As we analyse the Kingdom further we realise that the word kingdom can be understood in different ways.

Authority Exercised by a King

Both the word *baileia,* the Greek word translated kingdom, and the Hebrew word *malkuth* signify the rank and authority exercised by a king. Our present thinking deals with the people who are under the king's authority or the actual territory over which kingly authority is exercised. **So the nature of the authority may be closer to the understanding of the biblical concept of kingdom than the actual subjects of the authority.**

Psalm 145:13 expresses in poetic terms something of this idea, *"Thy kingdom is an everlasting kingdom, and thy dominion endureth throughout all generations."* In classical Hebrew poetry, the two verses of the poem are to express the same idea in differing ways. Therefore the poet's concept of the Kingdom was that it was God's actual dominion.

Take for instance King Herod – a.k.a. "Herod the Great!" - the unpopular king of Israel. Although he rebuilt the temple to majestic grandeur and built a great many fine public buildings in Jerusalem, he had no real kingdom. **There was no genuine basis for his authority** apart from Roman might. He had gone to Rome and had been given the kingship over Israel without a legitimate basis for having this kind of authority.

He was not born to it. A recognised Prophet did not anoint him. **He was not a descendant of Judah. He had no legitimacy. Although he lived in a palace, wore a crown and was called King Herod, his kingdom was bought and not earned.**

In Great Britain there are estates that can be bought which will carry a title with them. So if you have enough money, you may buy a title. Yet, this is not the same as being given a title by the queen, or being born into a noble family. **Money might buy you a title, but that title is not legitimate.**

On Earth and in Heaven

As we analyse this thinking further, it causes us to understand the prayer, which Jesus told us to pray: *"Thy kingdom come. Thy will be done in earth, as it is in heaven."* More than asking God to take over the world in a cataclysmic event, there seems to be the desire in the heart of the Lord for the authority of God to be as obvious to the earth as it is obvious in heaven.

To conclude then, I personally believe that the Kingdom of God concerns the nature of His reign and His authority, genuine, indisputable and eternal! The reign of God is present, but it will also be in the future. God has always been in charge! He is the Creator of the earth and for that matter the entire universe. He is all-powerful.

However, in this human arena called earth, God has allowed Himself to be limited. Satan was given a realm of authority; he is the god of this present age. He has authority over this world's systems. His seat of authority is in the immediate atmosphere surrounding the world.

Nevertheless God provided an escape from the territory over which Satan rules or has authority. He provided Jesus Christ, the last Adam! Amen.

We are more than victorious,
Dr Alan

PRAYER FOR THE DAY

Father thank You for complete and utter victory through Christ Jesus! I gladly reserve my life for Your glory. I give myself to Your Kingdom. To Your rule and authority. In Jesus' Name.

CONFESSION OF THE DAY

Today I walk in the authority, power and rule of almighty God, because I seek first His Kingdom. I allow Him to govern my life. I am liberated; spirit, soul and body! I am no longer subject to the powers of darkness. I am no longer oppressed. Because the Son has set me free, I am free indeed. Glory be to God!

ENDNOTES:

1. "More than Numbers" by Paul Y. Cho, Copyright © 1984, Published by Word Publishing UK

2. This "Truth for the Journey" has been taken from: https://watchersofthe4kings.com

3. Scripture references marked KJV are taken from the King James Version of the Bible.

4. Scripture references marked RSV are taken from the Revised Standard Version of the Bible, copyright 1952 [2nd edition, 1971] by the Division of Christian Education of the National Council of the Churches of Christ in the United States of America. Used by permission. All rights reserved.

14❖

The Kingdom Reign of God

Truth for the Journey
12th October 2012 – Kingdom Right Now

Kingdom Perspective

Thy Kingdom come, Thy will be done, on earth as it is in heaven *(Matthew 6:10)*.

In a previous letter we looked at "knots" and how the New Testament referred to the Kingdom of God as being like a "net" *(Matthew 13:47)*. We looked briefly at the vital role of "knots" in a net and how they bring stability and strength. We talked about how each knot represented "divine relationships" or "contacts" within God's Kingdom by using this powerful statement: "Divine connections produce strong relationships that in turn develop and enhance God's Kingdom."

So in keeping with this emphasis on the Kingdom, let's move on to talk more about what the Kingdom really is all about. To begin with, when the bible refers to the "Kingdom of God," it is actually referring to the "reign" *(authority)* of God more than the "realm" over which He rules or over which His authority resides. In other words, it is more about His authority than anything else!

Modern day Vernacular

However in our modern day vernacular this has gotten a little lost, either in translation or in cultural references and we tend to assume that "kingdom" refers to a "place" or "territory" more than to "authority."

Clearly this makes it vital for us to correct our focus a little so that the true context is not lost and where we can properly adhere to the true meaning of "kingdom" as seen in scripture. That kingdom is essentially more to do with reigning, ruling and exercising authority than it is about the realm where that authority functions. I would say this is a far more dynamic concept. Much less passive! And it is within the New Testament that the predominant meaning of "Kingdom" was God's reign or rule; with any other meaning seldom used.

For instance if we were to say, "The Gospel of the Kingdom of God," this would best be understood as *"THE GOOD NEWS OF THE REIGN OF GOD."* The Gospel is the good news and the Kingdom is His reign. Hence the good news of His reign!

We must consider this and make it personal; His Kingdom is His rule, His authority and His government; therefore when we receive the Kingdom of God, we receive and accept, His government and rule over our lives and hearts. To solidify this concept, we can remember what Jesus said, that we must *"receive the kingdom of God like little children" (Mark 10:15).*

In other words, **we must receive the government of God over our lives in childlike trust,** because He has our best interests at heart. **Besides when He "governs" our lives, nothing else can!**

Consider this a Little Further

Every time we have prayed the "Lord's Prayer," we have actually petitioned God to "reign" over us, *"...thy kingdom come..." (Matthew 6:10 KJV)* The correct context being that "His will" must be obeyed on earth *(by men)* just as it is obeyed in heaven! Because when men obey Him and His will is done in this present life, then the Kingdom of God has already come! It is already here! It is upon us! And obedience is always the key to truly dwelling in the Kingdom of God.

If we truly live in the Kingdom of God NOW, by allowing Him to govern over us, this in turn must mean that we see the things of His Kingdom coming to pass, not occasionally but regularly and routinely.

We know that what is "normal" to the Kingdom of God, is not normal to this world *(healings and miracles)* but must be "common-place" to us!

When the bible was written, the hearers of the Gospel possessed this early understanding of *"kingdom,"* and had a better grasp of its meaning than we do today. When they heard that the Kingdom of God was at hand, they understood that it meant **God's authority was being restored to the earth and that to enter the Kingdom of Heaven meant entering God's reign and experiencing the benefits of this in our immediate lives. Or perhaps today we would say in "real-time" which simply means "right-now!" Religion always keeps God "out-there" somewhere, but He and the rule of His Kingdom is "right-here" and "right-now!"**

Kingdom Reign Now

Many preachers have told us that entering the "Kingdom of Heaven" means going to heaven when we die. While this is true, it leaves us with very little understanding of the purposes of God and His intentions for His Church. **Failure to preach and understand the "Kingdom" of God is the reason that few Christians live the life of "OVER-COMERS" today.**

It is when the Kingdom of God becomes a "present reality" and not just a "future hope," that mankind is able to enjoy the blessings of God's rule and reign in their individual lives. Where they enter the more "abundant" and "victorious" life that is promised in scripture, yet sadly is only enjoyed by a minority of Christians today. Those who enjoy true Kingdom benefits today are not some elite group who live opulent lifestyles, but rather those who have genuine *"...righteousness and peace and joy in the Holy Spirit,"* as mentioned in Romans 14:17. This IS the Kingdom of God!

This is not to say that there is no future realm when Christ returns, but it opens to us the marvellous possibility that He will return to a world where His reign is already well established. Not to the fractured and feeble Church we have become, that is divided and has lost its grasp on what the true biblical concept of the Kingdom really is.

When the Kingdom of God is proclaimed to the Church and by the Church, we will have returned to the original biblical truth of the matter. Even more importantly, we will be obeying the instruction of our King Jesus, **to proclaim the Gospel of the Kingdom of God, hastening the day of His return.**

The Kingdom of God is the only thing that Jesus ever called the "Gospel." Few people understand this. And the fact remains that if we fail to proclaim the "Gospel of the Kingdom," we are not actually obeying His instruction to preach the "Good News of God's reign and authority!"

The Government of God

This is the best news that anyone can ever hear, because it is God's only solution to all of man's ills. When we accept this "King Jesus" as the ultimate "ruler" of *every* aspect of our lives, then and only then can we truly experience **Kingdom living as it should be, which is a righteous, peaceful and joyful lifestyle in the presence of the Holy Spirit (*Romans 14:17*).**

As ambassadors of His Kingdom our role on this earth is to administer His Kingdom justice here, His rule, reign and righteousness. This is the role of every single believer, to reign spiritually and administer His spiritual justice in order to put into effect His Kingdom right here and right now.

To administer in the dictionary means to manage the affairs of, formally give out, and to apply. This explains our role quite well in contemporary terms, because we have to minister into our everyday circumstances simply by applying God's spiritual truth and spiritual laws. We do this without denying or breaching natural laws, in order to do things from a Kingdom perspective! BUT **the laws of God's Kingdom obviously supersede all others and we can apply these truths into the spiritual realm and let it take effect there.**

Remember that everything originates in the spiritual realm first anyway *(Genesis 1:1-2)* and has its eventual effect here on the earth.

Take for instance such scriptures as Matthew 6:10 for example, where it says, "...as it is in heaven" and in Matthew 18:18 especially in the Amplified version where it talks about binding and losing on earth, just as it already is in heaven. **We are enforcers who enforce the things of God** but in the spirit realm FIRST. Because **that's where the struggle is, it is a spiritual battle and not one of flesh and blood** *(Ephesians 6:12).*

There are places of course where preaching is illegal and believers are forced underground but traditionally this has not hindered the gospel, on the contrary that's often when it runs the fastest, spreads hardest and supersedes all obstacles. But this is another discussion altogether!

What we are talking about here is applying God's spiritual truth into the atmosphere, letting it supersedes all else; yet without breaching natural or political laws, to the best of our ability! Remember just being righteous in an unrighteous world is spiritual warfare in itself. We don't have to open our mouths and we create conflict just being here – spiritually speaking! Even our worship is warfare, because it creates an atmosphere that is "contrary" to the atmosphere of this world.

Therefore even before we open our mouths, we are not welcome! Anything we engage in is spiritual warfare! Our very presence on earth creates a contradiction and a conflict.

Essentially we represent a real and present resistance to evil – particularly when yielded to the Holy Spirit.

Dr Alan

PRAYER FOR THE DAY

Father Your Kingdom rule is my freedom. I lean upon You and not upon my own understanding. Take everything I have to give You, including myself, and use it for Your Glory. I rejoice to be part of Your Kingdom. Govern my life. Lead me by Your Spirit. Fill me with the power of Your Word. In Jesus' Name.

CONFESSION OF THE DAY

Today I take my place. I take dominion. I walk out the authority that God has given me, to govern and reign in this life, through His name. I only have authority because I am submitted to His authority.

ENDNOTES:

1. This "Truth for the Journey" has been taken from: https://
   watchersofthe4kings.com

2. Scripture references marked KJV are taken from the King James
   Version of the Bible.

15❖

A Mixed Lifestyle
Produces a Sterile Future

Truth for the Journey
14th July 2017 – Mixed Lifestyle

Spiritual Mixtures

We will discuss in today's letter the dangers of "Spiritual Mixtures;" something that I come across daily, not only on my own geographical doorstep but also when I travel around the world. In fact as I prepare to take to the skies yet again, I am more aware than ever of this growing - although not new - trend. Therefore it is with genuine concern that I say, *"dangerous mixtures - exist within the Body of Christ today."*

So as I explain below... I trust that today's letter will provide much food for thought and much inspiration, albeit a clear-headed topic! We must encourage ourselves to face what faces all of us today, toxic-mixtures. It exists not only in the Body of Christ of course, but in the world around us. From the food we eat to the air we breathe, there are toxic mixtures that influence us every day of our lives.

God Addresses Mixtures

We don't have room perhaps to discuss all of them here but dangerous mixtures exist. God addresses this subject of mixtures Himself in His Word as we will see below, but mixtures include the natural vs. supernatural, psychology vs. the Word of God, Holy vs. unholy spirit etc. We have to agree, that some things in life should just never be mixed; so let's read on and discover what scripture says regarding this.

First let's see where God first brings this issue out in the Old Testament. Where He warns His people against mixtures especially in Leviticus 19:19 where it says,

> *You shall keep My statutes. You shall not let your livestock breed with another kind. You shall not sow your field with **mixed seed**. Nor shall a garment of **mixed linen** and wool come upon you.*

So there are three specific things that God warns against which are:

1. *Breeding **mixed livestock***
2. *Sowing with **mixed seed***
3. *Wearing a **mixed garment***

Sowing with mixed seed, represents the "message" that we bring *(when partly in truth and partly in error)* and wearing mixed garments refers to our "lifestyles," *(partly scriptural and partly of this world)*. Whereas allowing livestock breed with livestock that is of an incompatible kind would be equivalent to a Christian ministry or group aligning itself with a group that is non-Christian.

Consider it this Way

Scripture speaks of an "unequal yoking" as seen here in 2 Corinthians 6:14-17 *(KJV)* **"Be ye not unequally yoked together with unbelievers: for what fellowship hath righteousness with unrighteousness? And what communion hath light with darkness? And what concord hath Christ with Belial? Or what part hath he that believeth with an infidel?** And what agreement hath the temple of God with idols? For ye are the temples of the living God; as God hath said, I will dwell in them, and walk in *them;* and I will be their God, and they shall be my people. **Wherefore come out from among them, and be ye separate,** saith the Lord, and touch not the unclean *thing;* and I will receive you..."

In fact we see clearly that God wants us to "separate" ourselves from the mix, backed up again by James 4:4 where it states, "... know ye not that the **friendship of the world is enmity with God? Whosoever therefore will be a friend of the world is the enemy of God"** *(KJV)*. Harsh words but when it comes to mixtures, how else do you remedy the mixture but to "separate" the ingredients?

For instance gold usually contains a variety of other metals and in order to "purify" the gold, in other words to take the other metals out, it must be heated and proven by fire.

Then and only then is it considered "pure" gold. Now of course there have been extremists in every generation who have incited hatred and ethnic "cleansing." In recent history there were the likes of Hitler *(with his ideological Aryan race)* and others more recent such as Rwanda, the Sudan and Bosnia.

But we are not discussing mixtures of race in this context; rather our discussion of mixtures is predominantly a spiritual context. The Old Testament saw much physical killing, concerning the nature of mixtures, but this represents a type and shadow of what occurs spiritually in the New Testament.

Dangerous relationships contain dangerous "mixtures" not just in marriage, but also in all relationships. In fact Amos warned, "Can two walk together, except they be agreed?" *(Amos 3:3 KJV)* Marriage is important in this context as scripture says, "'For this reason a man will leave his father and mother and be united to his wife, and the two will become one flesh'? So they are no longer two, but one. Therefore what God has joined together, **let man not separate"** *(Matthew 19:5-6).*

There is much to this mixture business, which practically affects every area of our lives. In fact we have become so accustomed to unnatural mixtures that we hardly notice them anymore. But let's continue...

Sterile or Barren

For instance, my father was a farmer and growing up on a farm meant that I had first-hand knowledge of farm life. Therefore I know that mixed breeding produces creatures that are *"STERILE" (infertile or barren!)* Take for example when a horse mates with a donkey - all that union can produce is a "sterile mule" which means that it will "never" re-produce. We could liken this to "mixed breeding" amongst Christians and the world - which too can only produce "sterility and unproductiveness." Where we wonder why our "projects" don't produce anything more than weariness!

Our fruit is minimal even though our labour is much. Why? **Check for the mixtures.** Check for the contamination. Perhaps we have become sterile and we never noticed the "mixture" in our lives - that produced it. We must be this real!

On a personal level, my wife and I have always been very selective and careful regarding what we allow into our home; whether through TV, video games and the like... and with growing children this can be very challenging; nevertheless challenge worth taking seriously because as the results are so life altering. In other words, as ministers of the gospel - none of us can afford a potent pulpit ministry while our home lives are sterile!

For example sterile children who have just enough of God and the world - to make them dangerous! With a mixture of spirits - secular and spiritual, humanistic and godly; needless to say this grieves the Spirit of God who is jealous for us and our children and their children! He will

139

not share us with the world! He wants us to be "fruitful" *not* "sterile."* Jesus said *"Herein is my Father glorified, **that ye bear much fruit"** (John 15:5-8).*

Is it possible to have a mixture of spirits? Yes of course, mixture exists on every level and this particularly refers to the condition where both the Holy Spirit and unholy spirits are in operation.

To see this let's look at King Saul who also operated in a mixture of spirits. We know that in one instance he would prophesy via the Holy Spirit yet in another instance prophesy via a demon. *(What a sober warning to all of us!)* As King for forty years along with being a successful military commander, *"spiritual mixture" became his final undoing.* During his lifetime, he knew what it was to consult with God, but on the last night of his life he consulted a witch; did this produce life or was it sterile? The answer lies in the fact that Saul committed suicide on the battlefield the very next day!

If we apply this to our own lives, every time we approach God it must "produce life" as it says in Galatians 6:7-8 (KJV).

> *Be not deceived; God is not mocked: for whatsoever a man soweth, that shall he also reap. For he that soweth to his flesh shall of the flesh **reap corruption;** but he that soweth to the Spirit shall of the Spirit **reap life everlasting.***

God does not Condone Mixtures

Perhaps this is a subject that average believers don't give much thought to. But in James 3:9-12 it clearly says, "With our tongues we praise our Lord and Father. Yet, with the same tongues we curse people, who were created in God's likeness. Praise and curses come from the same mouth. My brothers and sisters, this should not happen! Do clean and polluted water flow out of the same spring? My brothers and sisters, can a fig tree produce olives? Can a grapevine produce figs? In the same way, a pool of salt water can't produce fresh water" *(GW)*.

We must never cultivate spiritual mixtures in our lives. We are not talking mere variety, spontaneity, individuality or diversity; of course all that is healthy. But once again we are discussing spiritual mixtures. God Himself makes this topic clear continually throughout the bible both Old and New Testaments.

For instance even though we have the power and life and death in our tongues, and the opportunity to operate in either, God commands us to operate in one only as seen here in the Old Testament where God said, *"I call heaven and earth to record this day against you, that **I have set before you life and death, blessing and cursing: therefore choose life,** that both thou and thy seed may live" (Deuteronomy 30:19-20 KJV).* We still have the same choice. Life or death. His desire has not altered either. Choose life He said. There can be no mixture.

Even Jesus said "...you are neither cold nor hot. **I wish you were either one or the other!** So, because you are lukewarm - neither hot nor cold – I am about to spit you out of my mouth" *(Revelation 3:15-16).*

In fact according to scripture everything is a matter of life or death *(Deuteronomy 30:19-20; Proverbs 18:21),* truth or error, light or darkness, blessing or cursing and heaven or hell. And if God has truly translated us from one kingdom to another - out of darkness and into light, then we must not attempt to create grey zones! *(Colossians 1:12-13)*

In James 1:8 it says *"A double minded (double spirited) man is unstable in ALL his ways."* Therefore it is in our best interest to reject all forms of the mixture. In 1 Corinthians 1:10 we see Paul the Apostle exhorting the Corinthians to remain united *(avoiding spiritual mixtures)*, *"...speak the same thing ... be perfectly joined together in the same mind and in the same judgment."* Therefore it is exhaustively clear from the Old to the New Testament, that God apposes all mixtures and intends us to be single minded, hearted, tongued and spirited! *NO MIXTURES.*

Confusion and Division

Finally in closing, **the result of mixture is confusion and division.** For instance, where there is a mixed message, part true or part false, people can only respond in two ways. Some will see the good and focus on it, and therefore accept the bad. Some will focus on the bad, and therefore reject the good. Neither accomplishes God's purpose. Confusion brings division and that is exactly what happens in the church: *confusion then division.* And the devil has three major objectives: *to steal, to kill and to destroy;* one way to bring destruction is through spiritual chaos. However, *"God is not the author of confusion, but of peace..." (1 Corinthians 14:33)*

We must be determined to remain single minded in all that we do and avoid cultivating any mixtures in our lives.

God wants the best for us and mixtures will only rob us of the blessings that He has for our families, ministry or business. So in order to stay blessed or relevant in God's Kingdom, *we must stay free of the mix!*

Until the next one!
Dr Alan

PRAYER FOR THE DAY

Father thank You for helping me to walk and live in "one" direction; by Your Word and by Your Spirit. Your Word says, "...let your 'Yes' be 'Yes,' and your 'No,' 'No;' anything beyond this comes from the evil one" (Matthew 5:37; James 5:12). Therefore I simply say "Yes" to You and "No" to mixture. Help me walk this out in Jesus' Name.

CONFESSION OF THE DAY

You are pure and unadulterated. No shadow turning with you. No mixtures. You are complete; single minded. Your Words are pure, You are not double tongued! When I turn to You, I find You are the same; unaltered by my imperfections! Hallelujah.

ENDNOTES:

1. This "Truth for the Journey" has been taken from: https://watchersofthe4kings.com

2. Scripture references marked GW are taken from GOD'S WORD®, © 1995 God's Word to the Nations. Used by permission of Baker Publishing Group.

3. Scripture references marked KJV are taken from the King James Version of the Bible.

16❖

Self-Exaltation Denies Grace

Truth for the Journey
25th August 2017 – Grace LifeStyle

The Purpose of Grace

Does that mean we can live any old way we want? ...can we do anything that comes to mind? ...some acts of so-called freedom... destroy freedom... at one time the more you did just what you felt like doing... the worse your life became and the less freedom you had... And how much different is it now as you live in God's freedom, your lives healed and expansive in holiness? *(Romans 6:16-19 MSG)*

It is important to acknowledge that grace "empowers" not "pacifies!" Grace enables us to do what we are called to do and not just to sit on our morals thinking that we are exhausting the true purpose of grace! Grace means change; moving on towards holiness and righteous living as the above scripture states, **"How different is it now** as you live in God's freedom, **healed... and expansive in holiness..."** *(vs. 19)*

When God really touches our lives with His grace - there is change - everything is **"...different, healed and holy!"**

However as much as we have been given grace and are living by grace - we all still crave the things of the flesh, our fallen nature; sin and the world. Some Christians - even leaders - are ambitious and willingly usurp *(take-over, dominate)* the lives of others as they try and forge out a ministry for themselves. This is based upon a cocktail *(Mixtures)* of selfish-ambition and what they think they learnt at bible school, and not upon "divine impartation" or "divine patterns" from heaven *(see Hebrews 9:23; 8:5; Exodus 25:40; 26:30).*

Grace is Sufficient

Instead they need to lose their "ambition" and "text-book" approach; humble them selves before God and receive "revelation" by the Spirit, as Moses received his divine instruction and pattern on the mountain. There is no basis for anything without this! No matter how much research we do, and I am somebody who certainly values study - but not without the Spirit. **Without Him all study is "dead-letter."** In fact anything is dead without Him breathing on it and through it!

Then on the other hand there are some folks who are just so "relaxed" about grace - they think that it's like the cream between the sponge cakes - that softens every blow! However they fundamentally misunderstand the purpose of grace. Grace is to go "through" *(not escape!)* to overcome and to thrive *(not just dwell and survive!)* Grace always works hand in hand with faith, not fear. "Playing-things-safe" does nothing for God!

The Grace Life-Style

Then there are those who like to call themselves "grace-junkies" and I am okay with this in the context that we all need to be craving more of God's grace every single day - but grace is not a means to sin. It is a means to "live" for God. Grace is not even a means to escape conviction. For if we harden our hearts to the Holy Spirit's conviction in our lives - we eventually fall into sin anyway.

The grace life-style is different to grace just for salvation. We all need grace for salvation but we also need the grace life-style that takes us onto "maturity" and "effectiveness" for God. This includes purity and holiness. Ephesians 2:7-10 *(KJV)* says:

> *...the exceeding riches of his grace in his kindness toward us through Christ Jesus. For by grace are ye saved through faith; and that not of yourselves: it is the gift of God: Not of works, lest any man should boast. For we are his workmanship, **created in Christ Jesus unto good works, which God hath before ordained that we should walk in them...***

My emphasis today is not *(grace for)* salvation but that we have a job to do! Good works ordained by God that we should walk in them. Not living-it-up in the largest church we can find; enjoying the best worship available so we can "celebrate" the fact that we are saved each and every week but do nothing with it! This is not being active for God; this is still all about self!

The Work of Grace

However God ordained good works for us to do, this requires both forces of grace and faith to accomplish it. **Passively accepting truth is not living truth.** However once we start living in obedience we find this triggers obedience in others. *(Rebellion might seem "contagious"... but that's just fallen nature already prevalent in all of us from birth... what child ever needs to learn disobedience! It's inherent in fallen nature... all flesh is corrupt without Christ and is hard-wired to sin!)* We see this in the book of Revelations, that our testimony of faith and obedience also helps others to overcome *(see 12:11).*

When we talk of receiving a pattern from heaven, this is something that is available for all of us, we call this God's job-description for our lives, but this can only be received by faith. However there are many who are content with just pew-filling and have no intention of receiving any mandate from God. Their only interest is spectator-sport!

The only grace they want to receive is for salvation, but they are mistaken, because although grace can never be earned - it still must be worked! And faith without the works of grace is dead.

In order to receive this pattern from heaven we must believe and trust the Giver of the pattern, the vision, the blue print - that paints a picture for our future. Faith alone is how we receive it – *"because faith is the substance of things hoped for"* *(Hebrews 11:1).*

All this is the work of grace and to continually walk in grace we have to continually humble ourselves; yielding our lives to His will rather than our own - submitting to the things of the Holy Spirit. Therefore in this life we need to hear God - His grace, His pattern and His direction. Believing and trusting Him and acting upon His Word and being obedient to His will. We need to walk by His Word and in His Word. In other words a **lifestyle that reveals salvation and sanctification.**

A walk of righteousness and holiness and in subsequent Truth for the Journey's we will be taking a look at the subject of "righteousness."

We should no longer live a life where we expect God to bless anything we do regardless. In such an existence - repentance is not considered necessary! After all we are saved by grace and He knows all things anyhow! Listen, when repentance is no longer deemed necessary - neither is the cross *(God forbid!)*

Grace is Necessary

There are people today who are intimidated to talk about "repentance," because that might suggest that someone is in sin! In some circles it is almost a dirty word! How ridiculous.

Let me just affirm that if there is no longer any sin - as the psychologists of the world would have us believe - then where is the need for grace? **Yet grace is necessary and so is repentance;** there are some in the Body of Christ right now who are teaching grace in error. They don't think so of course. But then again the ditches on either side of the truth are very easy to fall into.

Besides the only people who benefit from the cross are those who recognise their sin and their need for repentance and salvation. Jesus said from the cross: *"Father forgive them for they don't know what they do" (Luke 23:34 NKJV).*

Those He was referring to did not understand but this did not reduce their need for forgiveness! Sin is sin. Call it for what it is, as Jesus did. There is nothing polite about it and there will be nothing polite about it on judgement day; but let's not forget that God's Word already judges us! If we live according to His Word, as our plumb line for everyday living - yes we shall be saved - but we will also live by holy standards and not by double standards!

In addition, it's not hard to see that stretching grace to its limits only encourages "hypocrisy" - which is in itself sin *(Romans 6:16-19).*

Therefore grace should be presented as a teaching on repentance that leads to purity *(life-style)* but is rather presented as a license for immorality and continuing in our sinful natures - with no repentance required. Something that is certainly not new or unique! This began some 2000 years ago in the early church; Jude wrote in 1:4 *(AMP),*

*For there are certain men who have crept in unnoticed, whose condemnation was predicted long ago, ungodly men, **who turn the grace of our God into lawlessness and wantonness, a license for immorality; and deny and disown our only Master and Lord Jesus Christ...***

If any sense of guilt is taken away - this only makes it easier for people to sin and feel justified about it! And all the time we justify our actions or our sin, God cannot help us deal with it, as we should. We still need God to point out our sin today. We still need the conviction of the Holy Spirit today *(2 Timothy 3:16 MSG)*. We are not trophy winners for just showing up! We are more than conquerors because of Christ, but this thing does not stop with His free gift. It only "begins" there...!

Grace Can be Denied!

To finish, if we are not walking in obedience, we are not really "in grace" or walking "by grace." Many are living natural lives trying to make things work for them. In such cases the role of the Holy Spirit is made obsolete! His rightful role is to lead - not vice-versa, regardless of circumstances. Today we tend to want everything now and throw spiritual tantrums if God does not give us what we want, when we want it - NOW - we have become like spoilt children!

Yet the grace life-style is what we all need; conscious of holiness and purity before God our Saviour - we are not just pictures on a wall, waiting to be admired, we are active members of the Body proving salvation to the world through our lifestyle - rather than disproving it - through our non-existent lifestyle.

151

Because those who are led by the Spirit of God are sons
of God. For you did not receive a spirit that makes you a
slave again to fear, but you received the Spirit of sonship.
And by him we cry, "Abba, Father."

(Romans 8:14-15)

Stay in His Presence,
Dr Alan

ENDNOTES:

1. This "Truth for the Journey" has been taken from: https://
    watchersofthe4kings.com

2. Scripture quotations marked AMP are taken from the Amplified®
    Bible, Copyright © 2015 by The Lockman Foundation. Used by
    permission. (www.Lockman.org)

3. Scripture references marked KJV are taken from the King James
    Version of the Bible.

4. Scripture quotations marked MSG are taken from The Message.
    Copyright © 1993, 1994, 1995, 1996, 2000, 2001, 2002. Used by
    permission of NavPress Publishing Group.

5. Scripture quotations marked NKJV are taken from the New King
    James Version®. Copyright © 1982 by Thomas Nelson, Inc. Used by
    permission. All rights reserved.

17❖

Promoting the Lord or Self!

Truth for the Journey
16th June 2017 – Prophetic Teaching

Trying to be Positive

People should think of us as servants of Christ and managers who are entrusted with God's mysteries. Managers are required to be trustworthy *(1 Corinthians 4:1-2 GW)*.

There are certain individuals today who assume that they are in leadership when in actual fact they have never legitimately qualified for such position; perhaps born from ego and hidden agenda more than the high calling of God! So how do we recognise such individuals without starting a witch-hunt? Well they are really quite easy to spot but having said that, what is obvious to the trained eye is not necessarily obvious to the untrained and therefore spiritually vulnerable.

To begin with they are made up of the type of individuals who have for one reason or another been around the church world for many years and have a good grip on Christian jargon and philosophy yet more out of head knowledge and learnt-behaviour than of genuine living connection with God!

Inadvertently they come to believe that they have in some way been automatically chosen to be a *voice* to the Church! They even suppose that they have some sort of special supernatural qualifications and are convinced that they have some "special insights" that we all need - along with "special authority" to bring "correction" *(remember it's the Apostle and Prophet's role to bring oversight and correction)* wherever they feel necessary - even to the body at large!

So we must not fail to ask them, *"Who are you and who has qualified you to be in such position?"* Once they open their mouths they usually reveal themselves!

To keep things positive let's look at what qualifies a leader rather than what doesn't. According to scripture, there are two major qualifications for leadership:

- **First** of all there must be fruit; **fruit of lifestyle** and then **fruit of ministry.**

- **Secondly** there must be **recognition and appointment** *(see Acts 5:1-11; 6:1-7; Ephesians 4:11).*

But first we must look for the fruits; it's okay having a big mouth, but where is the fruit? Here are some scriptures concerning the "fruit of lifestyle" *(Galatians 5:22; Romans 12:3; 1 Timothy 3:1-f; Titus 1:5-16).*

Consider Paul's Example

Paul the Apostle went through years of "testing" once he submitted himself to the leaders at Antioch.

They must first be tested; and then...let them serve...
(1 Timothy 3:10)

According to this particular scripture, once the "testing" part stops, the "serving" part begins! As Paul found out, this took considerable time.

It remains a fact today that in God's Kingdom the way up is always down and the greatest amongst us is the servant of all. It is only the world that glories in arrogance and "ostentatious crowd-pulling" *(entertaining never qualified anyone for leadership!)* **Someone with a servant's heart is not *showy or flamboyant* but humble.** This is a good sign of leadership quality. In fact, for anyone who has genuinely been called to a leadership position within the Body of Christ, one of **the first things that the Holy Spirit is going to deal with is ...***ego!*

Yet as first mentioned above, certain individuals have the ability to "learn behaviour" that seems to be humble when in actual fact it is known as "false-humility." Perhaps we have become so familiar with the false that we no longer recognise the true. True humility is *often* misinterpreted. Therefore the

Spirit MUST lead us, without Him we are spiritually dull and cannot see. We have eyes to see and yet cannot see; ears to hear but cannot hear. Only the Holy Spirit can REVEAL all truth to us and keep us spiritually alert *(John 16:13).*

He is the Father's complete provision for us - so that we cannot be so easily misled. But if we choose to walk without Him, to be vulnerable and spiritually ignorant, then no one can be blamed but ourselves! Yet we are meant to be "Over-Comers" in Christ, not gullible or easily led astray, but spiritual laziness is often the cause of dullness *(see apostasy).*

Separated and Set Apart

Now let us emphasise on the fact that **all potential leaders are "separated" or "set apart" by God** *(it is never a natural selection, as seen in 1 Samuel 16:7)* and this "separation" actually means *"chosen."* Jesus Himself said, *"Many are called, but few are chosen..." (Matthew 22:14),* meaning that not many make it through the *"testing"* part! Yet the few who do are successfully "separated" unto the Lord *(so not everyone who claims to be a leader, is one!)*

While many want the nametag of "leadership" not many want the "costs" or "associated risks!" And while the "separating process" was never intended to be easy, according to scripture, anyone caught "shortcutting" is not legitimate! *(John 10:7; Matthew 7:13)*

Now let's take it a step further, **there are "offices" and "positions of service"** mentioned in the bible, *(1 Corinthians 12:28).*

*And God has appointed these in the church: first apostles,
second prophets, third teachers, after that ... helps...*

Once again notice that during those first years in Antioch
Paul did *not* occupy a "fivefold-office" *(see Ephesians 4:11)*
but instead served in the ministry of helps, only then did he
progress to the office of "Teacher" *(see 2 Timothy 1:11; Acts
13:1).*

John Bevere in his book "Thus Saith the Lord," says,
"Not only would Paul be tested in the realm of helps but
in the office of Teacher as well. When Paul was promoted
from Teacher to Apostle we again see how God chooses
and separates those that He wants to fill certain offices or
positions."[1]

In Acts 13:1-2 we can see how Paul was listed along with
other Teachers in Antioch and how the Holy Spirit wanted
them to be **specifically separated** unto Him. The appointed
time had finally come, the one who had been called to be an
Apostle all those years earlier on the road to Damascus in
Acts 9:15 had finally, after many years *(possibly 14 years)* of
testing and loyal service, been **successfully separated unto
God to be an Apostle.**

First he was **"called"** then served in the ministry of
"helps," then he progressed to the office of a **"Teacher"**
and finally the office of an **"Apostle."** Why? The reason:
Paul was faithful to promote the Lord and not himself *(see
1 Corinthians 4:2).*

Remember life is a progression of steps!
Dr Alan

PRAYER FOR THE DAY

*Father today I worship you for TRUTH. Thank you that I am not dull but alert! I am not easily deceived but easily "led" of YOUR SPIRIT and not by the spirit of this world. As You seek such to worship you, here I am Father - ready to worship! Let my humility be true and not false. Teach me Your ways so that the fruit of my lifestyle and the fruit of my ministry will not just reveal who I am but ultimately who You are. (In John 15:8 Jesus said, "Herein is my Father glorified that you bear much fruit, so shall ye be my disciples") **In Jesus' Name.***

CONFESSION OF THE DAY

Today the position that I seek more than any other is to be in the bosom of God; to have that "living-connection" with Him and to know Him as He can be truly known. I lay everything down - so that He alone can pick me up. The way up is down. Let Your Kingdom be truly established in my life and Your will be done (above mine) forever. Hallelujah!

ENDNOTES:

1. "Thus Saith the Lord?" by John Bevere, p120, Copyright © 1999, Published by Creation House, A Division of Strang Communications Company, Florida USA

2. This "Truth for the Journey" has been taken from: https://watchersofthe4kings.com

3. Scripture references marked GW are taken from GOD'S WORD®, © 1995 God's Word to the Nations. Used by permission of Baker Publishing Group.

18❖

Let's Come Back to Jesus

Truth for the Journey
15th September 2017 – Prophetic Teaching

There is Only One Way to Heaven

Now let's look at what it means to be Born-Again. This happens when we ask Jesus Christ to come into our lives as our Lord and Saviour – *(John 3:3, 5-8, 15-21 KJVS).*

*Jesus answered and said unto him, Verily, verily, I say unto thee, Except a man be **born again,** he cannot see the kingdom of God... Verily, verily, I say unto thee, Except a man be born of water and of the Spirit, he cannot enter into the kingdom of God. That which is born of the flesh is flesh; and that which is **born of the Spirit** is spirit. **Marvel not that I said unto thee, Ye must be born again.** The* *wind bloweth where it listeth, and thou hearest the sound thereof, but canst not tell whence it cometh, and whither it goeth: so is every one that is **born of the Spirit...***

*That whosoever believeth in him should not perish, but have eternal life. For God so loved the world, that he gave his only begotten Son, that whosoever believeth in him should not perish, but have everlasting life. **For God sent not his Son into the world to condemn the world; but that the world through him might be saved.***

*He that believeth on him is not condemned: but he that believeth not is condemned already, because he hath not believed in the name of the only begotten Son of God. And this is the condemnation, that light is come into the world, and men loved darkness rather than light, because their deeds were evil. For every one that doeth evil hateth the light, neither cometh to the light, lest his deeds should be reproved. **But he that doeth truth cometh to the light, that his deeds may be made manifest, that they are wrought in God.***

The True Sons of God and our Free Will

However the same bible that tell us, "For by grace are ye saved through faith; and that not of yourselves: it is the gift of God: Not of works, lest any man should boast" *(Ephesians 2:8-9 KJVS);* also tells us, "Work out your own salvation with fear and trembling" *(Philippians 2:12 KJVS).*

This is because grace doesn't negate personal responsibility, "He that hath my commandments, **and keepeth them,** he it is that loveth me: and he that loveth me shall be loved of my Father, and I will love him, and will manifest myself to him" *(John 14:21 KJVS)*.

Yes salvation is by grace through faith, but this doesn't make repentance redundant either. Jesus preached repentance and the Kingdom of God. True Christianity is a life of obedience, in the pursuit of true maturity, without an orphan spirit:

> *For as many as are led by the Spirit of God, they are the sons of God. For ye have not received the spirit of bondage again to fear; but ye have received the **Spirit of adoption, whereby we cry, Abba, Father.** The Spirit itself beareth witness with our spirit, that we are the children of God.*
>
> *(Romans 8:14-16 KJVS)*

Sanctification is a process, therefore there's none of us who aren't still a *"work in progress!"* And since sin is conceived in our souls and not in our spirits, the soul acts like a pendulum, swinging between the spirit and the flesh. Why? Because having a free-will means the choice is always ours, "I have set before you life and death, blessing and cursing: **therefore choose life...**" *(Deuteronomy 30:19 KJVS)*

"Father, if thou be willing, remove this cup from me: nevertheless **not my will, but thine, be done**" *(Luke 22:42 KJVS)*. In this very instance Jesus demonstrated a *surrendered* free will.

So our flesh is not born again, it's perishing and getting older. We don't get a new body until we receive our resurrection bodies: *(Philippians 3:21; 1 Corinthians 15:35; Revelation 21:4; 1 Corinthians 15:43, 44, 53).*

> *It is the same with the resurrection of the dead. What is sown is perishable, what is raised is imperishable.*
> *(1 Corinthians 15:42 NET)*

Eternal Way Maker

Christ died on the cross so that we could be forgiven and the temple veil was torn in two, symbolising access was granted to the Holy of Holies. Jesus is our eternal Way Maker. "I am the way, the truth, and the life: no man cometh unto the Father, but by me" *(John 14:6 KJVS)*.

Our soul and flesh benefit from God's indwelling presence in our lives. We are earthen vessels, who have been broken before Him, so that He can minister to us and through us.

Why broken? Let me make it very clear, the flesh is wicked: "The heart is deceitful above all things, and desperately wicked: who can know it?" *(Jeremiah 17:9 KJVS)*

Understanding vs. Vain Imaginations

> *When they knew God, they glorified him not as God, neither were thankful; but **became vain in their imaginations**, and their foolish heart was darkened.*
> *(Romans 1:21 KJVS)*

I have always enjoyed the way that Smith Wigglesworth described faith. And I have quoted him below. But **let us**

not be accused, in this generation, of wanting the *things* **of Christ without wanting Christ in person;** of worshiping our own imaginations and striving to *get* and *accumulate* things rather than taking up our crosses daily and letting Him take the wheel.

If we *must* be **ambitious** for anything, let it be **for truth and understanding.** Especially understanding: **"With all thy getting get understanding,"** *(Proverbs 4:7 KJVS);* "Buy *(pay the price of time, push into, study)* the truth, and sell it not; also wisdom, and instruction, and understanding" *(Proverbs 23:23 KJVS).*

The context for this is that we must have a foundation of knowledge for everything that we say. As preachers, we must never just preach what we *think,* anyone can *think!* We must go beyond mere *thinking.* Instead we must say what we *know,* not just what we *think.* And base nothing on wild assumptions, vain imaginations, not even educated guesses.

> *Let go of your own thoughts, and take the thoughts of God, the Word of God.* ***If you build yourself on imaginations you will go wrong.*** *You have the Word of God and it's enough.*
>
> *-- Smith Wigglesworth*

Knowing God by His Word

All lack of faith is due to not feeding on God's Word.
You need it every day. Feed on the living Christ of whom this Word is full. As you get taken up with the glorious fact and the wondrous presence of the living Christ, ***the faith of God will spring up within you.***

If I am going to know God, I am going to know him by His Word. *I know I shall be in heaven, but I could not build on my feeling that I am going to heaven. I am going to heaven because God's Word says it and I believe God's Word.* *"Faith comes by hearing and hearing by the Word of God."*

-- *Smith Wigglesworth*[1]

Let us work in the revelation of who we are as sons.
Dr Alan

ENDNOTES:

1. "Greater Works: Experiencing God's Power" by Smith Wigglesworth, Copyright © 2000, Published by Whitaker House, Pennsylvania USA

2. This "Truth for the Journey" has been taken from: https://watchersofthe4kings.com

3. Scripture references marked KJV are taken from the King James Version of the Bible.

4. Scripture quotations marked NET are taken from the NET Bible® Copyright ©1996-2006 by Biblical Studies Press, L.L.C. http://netbible.com All rights reserved.

19❖

His Amazing Love
Has Set the Captive Free!

Truth for the Journey
1st April 2021 – Amazing Love

Death is Conquered, Victory Secured

Jesus shared our humanity *completely*. Temptation was not far from Him, yet He never sinned. Death He tasted, but not for Himself. In fact, He had no reason to die, were it just for Himself, because He was **without sin** *(2 Corinthians 5:21)*. The only reason Christ died was for the sake of humanity – who were the true recipients of punishment, worthy of death, because of their sins against God.

*Since the children have flesh and blood, he too **shared in their humanity** so that by his death he might destroy him* *who holds the power of death – that is, the devil - and free those who all their lives were held in slavery by their fear of death.*

(Hebrews 2:14-15)

Judgement rested heavily upon humanity and could not be averted. Sin had to be punished by death; **blood** had to be shed. Our God is merciful, but He is also **just.** Jesus satisfied every requirement; dying a *sinless* death. *Eternal separation* was the verdict passed against humanity – but Jesus appealed on the grounds of His **Blood** and won the case – *which will never be overruled! (see Isaiah 9:7)*

The End Of Fear
Infirmity no Longer has a Hold

Isaiah prophesied Jesus' victory over disease and sickness: *"This was to fulfil what was spoken through the prophet Isaiah: 'He took up our infirmities and carried our diseases'"* (Matthew 8:17). In Matthew chapter 4:24 it says, that Jesus healed all who were brought to Him. During His ministry on earth, Jesus demonstrated the Father's love by healing their infirmities. Love desires that *none should perish but have everlasting life (John 3:16).*

The condition of our spirit, soul and body is of importance to God *(1 Thessalonians 5:23).* Jesus didn't merely take our sin to the cross, but also our infirmities and diseases. *"By his wounds we are healed" (Isaiah 53:5).* John 4:34 says that Jesus came to do the will of the Father; *"to do the will of Him who sent me."* It is the Father's will that you be saved and healed and that you receive every spiritual blessing *(Ephesians 1:3-14).*

Jesus did all that was necessary to see that the will of His Father was fulfilled; *...and to finish His work*. That's why Jesus could declare from the cross before He died, *"it is finished"* *(John 19:30)*.

The Work of the Cross-is Complete

When all was accomplished, Jesus ascended to His Father's side, yet there was no closure! His work continues! He lives forever to minister in the presence of God on our behalf, interceding for us continually *(see Romans 8:34)*.

And when God the Father sees Jesus, He sees us, as we are *"...seated in heavenly places in Christ Jesus"* (Ephesians 2:6). Imagine this: if the Father sees Christ continually before His face, we are also seen continually! Each time He sees us, He sees Christ; each time He sees Christ, He sees us. **Reconciled forever;** eternally-found in Christ Jesus.

> *Who shall separate us from the love of Christ? Shall trouble or hardship...?*
>
> *(Romans 8:35)*

So, God the Father always sees us **together!** Under the **Blood,** nothing can separate us! When He looks upon us, He not only sees Christ or us but He also sees His **Covenant.** We are eternal reminders, found continually before His throne – **in Christ Jesus.**

That's why Romans 8:1-4 says that the only ones who are free from condemnation are those who are **in Christ Jesus.** Those in condemnation *(of the flesh)* cannot stand before the throne of God, only those who are **in Christ Jesus,** *...according* *to the Spirit.* Outside of Christ we look like **sin,** but **in Christ** we actually look like Him!

We Used To Look Like Sin Now We Look Like Him! **You Will never be Denied**

Because Jesus is your faithful High Priest, who *...lives always to intercede for you,* according to Hebrews 7:25, you will never be denied when you enter into God's presence. This free passage and unlimited access to the throne afforded you by the cross, allows you unrestrained favour before God, as long as you **remain in Christ.** Jesus underwent such terrible suffering, for a special purpose, and that was to make us holy, as He is holy *(1 Peter 1:16).*

> *Jesus...**suffered...to make the people holy** through his own Blood.*
>
> *(Hebrews 13:12)*

He Suffered To Make Us Holy **His Ever Faithful Love**

God is the same yesterday, today and forever, and there is no shadow of turning with Him. His love remains constant throughout the generations. Because we witnessed the faithfulness of Christ towards His Father – staying true to His will under all circumstances – we know that without failure or compromise Jesus will remain faithful to us! He is unable to change, He forever remains the same. His Love has been tested and proven to be **unconditional!**

It all rests on who **He is,** as 1 John 4:7-21 declares, *God is Love,* and 1 Corinthians 13:8 reminds us that *Love never* *fails.* **God's love** is **never** based on anything we have done. It is only ever based upon what Jesus accomplished, for yesterday, today and forever. *"I think that if there could be one sight more wonderful than the Love of Christ,"* said Charles H. Spurgeon, *"it would be the **Blood** of Christ."*

So Much Talk Of His Blood Yet So Little Is Understood!

Spurgeon goes on to say, "I do not know of anything more divine. It seems to me as if all the eternal purposes worked up to the Blood of the Cross, and then worked from the **Blood** of the cross towards the sublime consummation of all things. Oh, to think that He should become man!

God has made spirit, pure spirit, embodied spirit; and then materialism; and somehow, as if He would take all up into one, the Godhead links Himself with the material. He then wears dust about Him even as we wear it; and taking it all up, He then goes, and in that fashion, redeems His people from all the evil of their soul, their spirit, and their body, by the pouring out of a life, which while it was human, was so in connection with the divine, that we speak correctly of 'the **Blood** of God.'

Turn to the twentieth chapter of the Acts, and read how the Apostle Paul puts it: *'Feed the church of God, which he hath purchased with his own **Blood**.'* I believe that Dr Watts is not wrong when he says – *'God that loved and died.'* **It is an incorrect accuracy, a strictly absolute accuracy of incorrectness!**

So it must be ever when the finite talks of the Infinite. It was a wonderful sacrifice that could absolutely obliterate, annihilate, and extinguish sin, and all the traces that could possibly remain of it; for *'He hath finished the transgression, made an end of sins, made reconciliation for iniquity, and brought in everlasting righteousness.'*

Ah, dear friends! You have seen this, have you not? But you have to see more of it yet; and when we get to heaven, we shall then know what that **Blood** means, and with what vigour shall we sing..." *(Morgan and Spurgeon 345-347).*

He Loved Us And Washed Us In His Own Blood!

Amen,
Dr Alan

ENDNOTES:

1. Taken from "His Life is in the Blood" by Dr Alan Pateman, pages 20-25, Copyright © 2007, Second Print 2017, Published by APMI Publications

20❖

The Winner's Life

Truth for the Journey
25th June 2021 – Apostolic Teaching

Winning in Life through a Winning Mind

For as he thinketh in his heart, so *is* he... *(Proverbs 23:7 KJV)*

I love to see people succeed in life, just like the artist treasures his painting and the craftsman his violin, so our Creator cherishes His design! He is concerned about our dreams, goals and our ability to be happy and to enjoy life. But all said and done, none of us can truly enjoy life unless we STAY IN OUR RIGHT MINDS!

Success is being happy. Happiness is basically feeling good about our lives and our plans.

Two forces are vital to happiness: our Relationships and our Achievements.

The Gospel also has two forces: the Person of Jesus Christ, and the principles He taught. One is the Son of God, the other is the system of God. One is the life of God, the other is the law of God. One is the King, the other is the Kingdom. One is an experience with God, the other is the expertise of God. One is heart-related, the other is mind-related.

Salvation is experienced *"instantaneously"* while God's wisdom principles are learned *"progressively,"* and both are essential for success and happiness.

In everything therefore we must make it a priority to protect our thought lives. Some folks like to shout about their "double portion" but have never dealt with their fanatic in the attic! In reality the same Holy Spirit will make us deal with this chief opponent *first;* there is no uncertainty about it, we must conquer our minds!

This is a place where there can be no demilitarized zone, no middle ground. Either it belongs to the enemy or to God. When it comes to the mind there is no grey fudge. It is black or white, all or nothing. Another thing is for certain, where there is no discipline there is no Holy Spirit! He is never chaos. He is always order! Anyone who is successful today *(whether secular or Christian)* is someone who has mastered his or her minds with sheer "discipline." From businessmen to politicians, sports personnel or record breakers, they set their "minds" on a goal and don't deviate.

Sadly in retrospect many Christians are incapacitated *(out of action!)* because they have never learnt how to protect their thought lives. Satan bombards them with fear, hatred, suspicion depression, mistrust and a host of other mental distractions *or should I say disorders.*

But why does this "zone" have to be the most vulnerable area of our lives, because happiness really does begin between our ears. The mind is the drawing room for tomorrow's successes or failures; what happens there *(in our minds)* happens in time. As scripture clearly tells us *"...as he thinketh in his heart, so is he" (Proverbs 23:7 KJV).* So what you "keep in mind" from day to day is really what is shaping your future - positive or negative.

Making "mind-management" a MUST for any believer who seeks to be an over-comer. In fact it's not hard to recognise an over-comer from an defeatist; simply someone who is self adjusting vs. someone who lives in perpetual internal chaos and confusion. And their outer world usually shows it too.

Be Transformed

Our mind must be renewed. God's salvation includes the mind. Conquering or mastering the mind can be called *renewing the mind,* which is why Paul wrote to the Romans saying:

> *Do not conform any longer to the pattern of this world, but be transformed by the renewing of your mind. Then you will be able to test and approve what God's will is - his good, pleasing and perfect will.*
>
> *(Romans 12:2)*

The late Dr Bob Gordon said, "The mind is a veritable battlefield in the experience of many people. Lack of mental discipline leads to chaos in the thought life, an inability to discern truth from error and bondage to an imagination that is able to breed negative ideas, dreams, visions and bogey men quicker than they can be recognised. This is why Paul writes to the Romans: 'Do not conform any longer to the pattern of this world but be transformed by the renewing of your mind' *(Romans 12:2)*. Certain steps are needed to close the mind to Satan's influence and to release it to be used by God."

He goes on to say that we must adopt a proper attitude towards our old life: "What I mean by this is that we should be taking the position with regard to our old nature in the death of Christ. It was to break the power and bondage of the old nature that Jesus died: 'In the same way, count yourselves dead to sin but alive to God in Christ Jesus' *(Romans 6:11)*. We need to live under a new landlord. The flesh has no legal right to make its demands upon us: 'Therefore, brothers, we have an obligation - but it is not to the sinful nature, to live according to it' *(Romans 8:12)*.

Time and again we are presented with these 'moral imperatives' of the Holy Spirit in scripture. It is quite clear that the man of the Spirit has been given a new authority in Christ which he can exercise against the negative spiritual power of the flesh."[1]

Therefore my friends, I urge you in view of God's mercy upon your life, offer your lives, ministries as a living sacrifice that He may be lifted up.

Dr Alan

ENDNOTES:

1. "Understanding the Way" by Bob Gordon, pages 260, 266, Copyright © 1987, Published by Marshall Morgan and Scott, Marshall Pickering, UK

2. This "Truth for the Journey" has been taken from: https://watchersofthe4kings.com

3. Scripture references marked KJV are taken from the King James Version of the Bible.

21 ❖

The Battlefield

Truth for the Journey
29th June 2021 – Apostolic Teaching

The Battle Ground is the Mind

In her bestseller, *"The Battlefield of the Mind"* Joyce Meyer also states that there is a war going on where our minds are the battlefield, the good news being that God is fighting on our side! Joyce uncovers the tactics of the enemy and gives a clear-cut plan to triumph in the fight for your mind.

She teaches how to renew the mind through the Word and stand victoriously in the battlefield of the mind. Our enemy uses a deliberately devised plan of deceit and lies, attacking our minds with doubting thoughts, fear and paranoia to erode our resistance; investing any amount of time in order to defeat us.

However the Word of God has the power to cleanse our minds regardless remembering it is all-important that we read and meditate on His Word, remaining obedient to it. We must read, meditate and speak the Word continually, taking captive every thought to make it obedient to Christ (2 Corinthians 10:5).

> *Do not let this book of the law depart from your mouth; meditate on it day and night, so that you may be careful to do everything written in it. Then you will be prosperous and successful.*
>
> *(Joshua 1:8)*

The following scriptures reveal the weaknesses of our Natural mind:

1. It is hostile to God *(Romans 8:5-7):* unbelievers are often "hostile" towards the gospel.
2. The things of God are foolish to the natural mind: *(1 Corinthians 2:12-14)*
3. The natural mind is blinded to God by Satan: *(2 Corinthians 4:4)*
4. The natural mind is the source of violent and evil desires: *(Ephesians 2:3)*
5. The natural mind is futile in its thinking and darkened in its understanding: *(Ephesians 4:17-18)*

Discerning your Thoughts

Perhaps you can imagine how Joshua might have felt after he had just successfully crossed over the Jordan River, through an awesome act of faith, which took him and all the people across, only to arrive in Jericho to look up and see those gigantic walls that surrounded that great city *(Joshua 1:2; 5:13)*.

As a military man his mind must have gone to work strategizing, *"Well if we build some ramps, we'll come at it like this... we can make a hole and maybe get through..."* But instead of attacking the walls, God's instructions was to "march" around it in silence for seven long and probably hot days - surely this sounded so foolish to Joshua's naturally military mind.

Joshua was as natural as you or I; it would have been as much of a discipline for him as it is for us to learn to stop thinking with the natural mind. Being disciplined enough to flow with the mind of God, especially when the instructions seemed so completely "un-natural" and out of sync with his natural instincts! A military figure had to lay his own strategy down in order to accept the Lord's.

This is not always easy, but then submission rarely is; it's based on trust, faith, relationship AND dying to self.

Joshua had already given several promises and instructions:

1. His promises are about to be fulfilled
2. Your territory will extend
3. No one will be able to stand up against you
4. I will never leave you nor forsake you
5. Be strong and courageous
6. Be careful to obey

7. Do not let this Book of the Law depart from your mouth
8. Get your supplies ready
9. When you see the ark of the covenant *(Holy Spirit)* follow it
10. Consecrate yourselves *(sanctification and holiness)*

But on the Seventh Day

Then the Lord showed up as commander and said, this is Holy Ground, I have delivered Jericho into your hands. Then they all marched around in obedience seven times "shouting and praising" the Lord, it was then and only then - out of sheer faith of obedience and discipline - that the walls came tumbling down.

Let's be honest, it takes a disciplined mind just to keep our mouths quiet! "For out of the abundance *(overflow)* of the heart, his mouth speaks!" *(Luke 6:45 AMP)*

Finally remember this, faith is not chatty or spontaneous, it's too deliberate! And disciplining our minds has to be a determined - on purpose and deliberate - act of our faith. Only this will get the job done, no matter how long it takes. Then and only then can we truly say that we have conquered our own minds by allowing "the mind of Christ" *(1 Corinthians 2:16)*.

Dr Alan

ENDNOTES:

1. "The Battlefield of the Mind" by Joyce Meyer, Copyright © 1995, Published by Harrison House, Inc. USA

2. This "Truth for the Journey" has been taken from: https://watchersofthe4kings.com

3. Scripture quotations marked AMP are taken from the Amplified® Bible, Copyright © 2015 by The Lockman Foundation. Used by permission. (www.Lockman.org)

22 ❖

Forces Influencing Society

Truth for the Journey
4th August 2017 – Watchers Letter

Discipling all Nations

He who overcomes... I will give him authority and power OVER THE NATIONS *(Revelation 2:26 AMPC).*

Why are the NATIONS so significant to God? Clearly the Great Commission is not just about building churches but "discipling all nations." How then do we do this and is the Church succeeding in this mandate?

Different vying forces are influencing society today, in an endless power struggle. Whether bombastic or subtle, the stimuli are real. In recent times this battle is often referred to as "culture wars," which basically involves, *"conflict between distinctive groups that hold different ideals, beliefs and philosophies."*

The different realms these struggles manifest, include such areas as, the economy, entertainment and religion, which all have strong power structures that attempt to shape society according to specific agendas. Such forces compete for mastery.

Dominating Characteristics

That's why certain areas have dominating characteristics, such as commerce in New York City, religion in Rome and entertainment in Los Vegas, *(quick example)*. Obviously there are more areas to societal structure than those I've just shortlisted, especially coming from a biblical perspective; let me explain:

> *Worthy is the Lamb that was slain to receive **power**, and **riches**, and **wisdom**, and **strength**, and **honour**, and **glory**, and **blessing**.*
>
> *(Revelation 5:12)*

When we speak of discipling the nations, we are speaking of the seven pillars or gateways of society, which correspond with the seven attributes mentioned above.

According to Johnny Enlow their parallels are as following:

Power = Government
Riches = Economy
Wisdom = Education

Strength = Family
Honour = Religion
Glory = The Arts *(Entertainment)*
Blessing = Media

We are to conquer and disciple each area for Christ and then deliver them unto Him, "The kingdoms of this world are become the kingdoms of our Lord, and of his Christ; and he shall reign forever and ever" *(Revelations 11:15)*.

This concept is not new of course, in the mid-70's the founder of, **"Youth With a Mission"** *(YWAM)* Loren Cunningham, and founder of **"Campus Crusade"** Bill Bright, were developing strategy surrounding the **"The Seven Mountains of Societal Influence."** They felt that their God-given mandate was to bring godly change to each nation by reaching its seven mountains of influence.

They understood that the **Great Commission** was not to build churches but to build people *(make disciples)*, in EVERY nation. Its like comparing apples and oranges, but I prefer *"pillar or gateway"* opposed to "mountain" when I'm teaching this subject, but it really doesn't make much difference. It's not a case of semantics, the concept is the same.

We must recognise that this heavenly mandate *already* rests on every generation:

*Go then and **make disciples of all the NATIONS,** baptizing them into the name of the Father and of the Son and of the Holy Spirit.*

(Matthew 28:19 AMPC)

For the Body of Christ to truly have an impact on what shapes the culture, it must first influence each of the seven major infrastructures, pillars or gateways, already mentioned: Media, Government, Education, Economy, Family, Religion and The Arts *(Entertainment)*.

Gateways in Societies

There are gateways in societies, in cities, countries and nations. These represent places of authority. In Proverbs 31 for example it says that, "Her husband is **known in the gates**," of the city. In addition to that, at the end in verse 31 it says "Let her own works praise her in the **gates**." If this represents the church, it proves the point that Jesus *(her husband)* wants his bride the church to have influence in the "city gates" and not to leave that up to the secular world to control such things. We must not be afraid to have influence in all these areas. This was always God's plan.

> *Her husband is **known in the gates**, when he sitteth among the elders of the land... Give her of the fruit of her hands; and let her own works praise her in the gates.*
> *(Proverbs 31:23, 31)*

Over the years and depending on who has been teaching this subject, they have been called "mountains," "pillars," "gateways," or even "walls" *(such as Jericho)*, in context with something that we must conquer. Regardless of names however, the revelation is the same.

We've talked for years about the "information gateways" and that if we capture those particular gateways, then we capture the city. It's strategic. I've always taught my students, **"Faith without strategy is dead!"**

This is a big issue. Just think. Those who seek ultimate control over peoples, cities, towns and nations, must do so by first controlling their access to information. It's a no brainer as far as I am concerned and it's been going on for generations, but none more so than now, when the proliferation of the Internet has presented real challenges to governments world wide.

In China for example, they discovered that trying to control the information outflow was virtually impossible, so instead they blocked it and created their own. Which is why YouTube, Facebook, Twitter and the like, have been blocked in China and replaced with such things as: WeChat, Baidu, RenRen, Youku, Weibo and others.

The Mission Field

In this vein, we can stop viewing things in terms of secular or non-secular and see each area that we are called into as the mission field and that Kingdom strategies are already in place and that God will prepare us for specific mission fields. For example each field has its adjoining spiritual warfare and we must be ready.

Those with the God-given mission to influence the economy through entrepreneurial innovation or stockbroking for example will need a specific preparation. Freedom from the spirit of mammon, greed or the love of money would have to be completely overcome on a personal level, if ever one hoped to overcome in that field.

Where we are compromised, that's where we fail. The "ites" in our personal promised land must be beaten, to avoid defeat on the wider mission field.

*As the Eternal, your True God, is bringing you into the land where you're going to live when you cross the Jordan, He'll drive out many nations ahead of you, **Hittites, Girgashites, Amorites, Canaanites, Perizzites, Hivites,** and **Jebusites,** seven nations that are bigger and stronger than you are.*

The Eternal your God will put them in your power. *You must crush them; destroy them completely!* ***Don't make any treaties with them,*** *and don't show them any mercy.*

(Deuteronomy 7:1-2 VOICE)

Each of the "-ites" mentioned above – **Hitt-ites, Girgash-ites, Amor-ites, Canaan-ites, Perizz-ites, Hiv-ites,** and **Jebus-ites,** obviously represent seven areas of spiritual warfare or oppression that we overcome as we pursue our God given mandate. This is something that I have been teaching for many years. These seven "–ites" coincide with the seven pillars or gateways that we are discussing here.

For now, let me say that there are *governing principalities* in each of the seven areas that will perceive us as hostiles and not as friendlies! The battle will rage and unless our motives are pure, we will be forced into quick retreat. Our only leverage is God and His *pattern*. Our success is totally reliant on our full compliance:

I seek not mine own will, but the will of the Father which hath sent me. ... I came down from heaven, not to do mine own will, but the will of him that sent me.

(John 5:30; 6:38 KJVS)

We are not like dangerous free radicals that disrupt the body and cause disease and dysfunction; instead we are of the breed that grasps the beneficial dynamics of divine-cooperation.

Navy Seals, once their mission objectives are set, their training and stick-to-it-ive-ness fulfils the mission at all costs. Our security is in our training and God's instruction. His favour and power meet us on the job, He is equal-to-and-much-more-than anything that we will ever face.

So, like Moses we must follow and obey heaven's instructions to the ninth degree, building according to heaven's pattern and not ours: "Look that thou make them after their **pattern,** which was shewed thee in the mount." "Study the **design** you were given on the mountain and make everything accordingly" *(Exodus 25:40 KJVS/MSG).*

Discipling the Nations

The word "nation" or "the nations," is mentioned hundreds of times throughout scripture *(over 300 times!)* God simply thinks bigger than we do. Considering that the Great Commission could have said, "make disciples of all church converts, souls or even men." Instead it uses "nations." Why is this significant?

According to the Strong's Concordance G1484 "nations" applies: *"a race (as of the same **habit**) that is a tribe; specifically a foreign (non-Jewish) one (usually by implication **pagan**): -* Gentile, heathen, people… the human family, tribe, group." Basically referring to anyone who is not already worshipping the one true God. It's all encompassing. No one slips the radar. God is no racist!

The commission includes everyone. No one is excluded. It includes every race, every tribe, every foreigner, every pagan, every gentile and heathen *(godless)*, everybody in the human family, every conceivable people group on earth. They all matter, no matter what their current habits or customs *(current culture)*. Think of it!

My interpretation of "all nations" in context with the Great Commission, refers to "ALL those who are currently outside of God," regardless of who they are and where they come from.

> *For God so loved the world, that he gave his only begotten Son, that whosoever believeth in him **should not perish, but have everlasting life.***
>
> *(John 3:16 KJV)*

> *The Lord is… **not willing that any should perish.***
> *(2 Peter 3:9 KJV)*

> *I give unto them eternal life; and they **shall never perish, neither shall any man pluck them out of my hand.***
> *(John 10:28 KJV)*

His Desire is for the Nations

Old Testament examples:

*Thou shalt be a father of many **nations**...*
(Genesis 17:4-6 KJV)

*Abraham shall surely become a great and mighty **nation**, and all the **nations** of the earth shall be blessed in him.*
(Genesis 18:18 KJV)

*Ask of Me, and I will give You the **nations**...*
(Psalm 2:8 AMPC)

*I have this day set thee over the **nations**...*
(Jeremiah 1:10 KJV)

*The **desire of all nations** shall come...*
(Haggai 2:7 KJV)

New Testament examples:

*My house shall be called of all **nations** the house of prayer...*
(Mark 11:17 KJV)

*In thee shall all **nations** be blessed.*
(Galatians 3:8 KJV)

*Who through faith subdued **kingdoms**...*
(Hebrews 11:33 KJV)

*To him will I give power over the **nations**.*
(Revelation 2:26 KJV)

*That he should deceive the **nations** no more...*
                    (Revelation 20:3 KJV)

*For the healing of the **nations.***
                    (Revelation 22:2 KJV)

Clearly our seven-fold mission is to disciple the "nations" using God's seven-fold strategy plan. Once captured for Jesus, these seven major culture-bending, society influencing pillars or spiritual gateways, will help us fulfil the Great Commission, given us in Matthew 28:19.

Dr Alan

ENDNOTES:

1. This "Truth for the Journey" has been taken from: https://watchersofthe4kings.com

2. Scripture references marked AMPC are taken from the Amplified® Bible (AMPC), Copyright © 1954, 1958, 1962, 1964, 1965, 1987 by The Lockman Foundation. Used by permission. www.Lockman.org

3. Scripture references marked KJV are taken from the King James Version of the Bible.

4. Scripture references marked KJVS are taken from the Strong's Concordance with KJV. Taken from the TecartaBible App, © 2017 Tecarta, Inc. Version 7.11.5. Used by permission. All rights reserved.

5. Scripture quotations marked MSG are taken from The Message. Copyright © 1993, 1994, 1995, 1996, 2000, 2001, 2002. Used by permission of NavPress Publishing Group.

6. Scripture quotations marked VOICE are taken from The Voice™. Copyright © 2008 by Ecclesia Bible Society. Used by permission. All rights reserved.

23❖

The Influence of Media

Truth for the Journey
13th October 2017 – Watchers Letter

Media of Fear

Hello and welcome to another Truth for the Journey. This is part one of an exciting subject, in regards to the implications of media and the influence that it has in society today. The scriptures are clear that this particular giant needs to be conquered, reversing the negatives that program us.

Let's start by examining Deuteronomy 7:1-2,

*When the Lord brings you into the Promised Land, as he soon will, he will destroy the following seven nations, all greater and mightier than you are: **the Hittites,** the*

Girgashites, the Amorites, the Canaanites, the Perizzites, the Hivites, the Jebusites. When the Lord your God delivers them over to you to be destroyed, do a complete job of it — ***don't make any treaties or show them mercy; utterly wipe them out.***

(Deuteronomy 7:1-2 TLB)

Today we are putting the spotlight on the Hittites, which is the first of seven nations mentioned above that represent seven major areas of influence that we must conquer. "He that overcometh shall inherit all things" *(Revelation 21:7 KJV)*.

Though scripture calls them *nations*, I'm going to refer to them as *spiritual gateways*. Now we are going to break down exactly what this spiritual gateway called "Hittite" actually stands for, so that we know what we are up against.

Conquering the Gateway of Fear & Terror

When God, your God, brings you into the country that you are about to enter and take over, he will clear out the superpowers that were there before you: [starting with] the HITTITE... Those seven nations are all bigger and stronger than you are. God, your God, will turn them over to you and you will conquer them.

(Deuteronomy 7:1-2 MSG, emphasis added)

The Eternal your God will put them in your power...

(Deuteronomy 7:2 VOICE)

Hebrew Definition of Hittite

Bearing in mind that Hebrew words are compound words, we must employ the aid of some great bible tools, such as the Strong's Hebrew Concordance and the Brown-Driver-Briggs' Lexicon, to give us a clear definition of "Hittite," *(which originates from the name "Heth,")* as seen in the bible.

Put in bite-sizes like this, the implications of this particular spiritual gateway are very clear: fear, terror and discouragement.

- **H2850 Hebrew: chittîy** *(khit-tee').*
- Hittite = "descendant of Heth." The nation descended from Heth, the 2nd son of Canaan; once inhabitants of central Anatolia *(modern Turkey),* later in north Lebanon

- **H2845 Hebrew: chêth** *(khayth).*
- Heth = "terror" - a son of Canaan and the progenitor of the Hittites

- **H2865 Hebrew: châthath** *(khaw-thath')*
- Heth = "terror." To *prostrate;* hence to *break down,* by violence or confusion and **fear.** To abolish, affright, make afraid, amaze, beat down, discourage, cause to dismay, go down, scare, terrify. To be shattered, scared and to terrify.

Who better to transport fear and terror, than the media? This spiritual gateway then represents media, which acts like a conduit that feeds negatives, propaganda into our lives and methodically looks to break us down. When we are continually stunned, confused and negative, that's when we are weakest.

If Satan can feed us with enough negatives daily, which we in turn run with, the rest of his dirty work is done for him. In other words, once we mount the hamster wheel of pessimism, which steadily gains momentum in our lives, it's very hard getting off!

The Media's Power to make us Negative

Media certainly has the power to wear us out with negatives, if we allow it. So we must develop a robust and impenetrable filter that protects us from the regular onslaughts of the media.

Appreciate that without the media's cooperation, things like terrorism would have no echo chamber to work with. The noise of their threats, and the images of their destruction would go largely unnoticed, and yet they continue unopposed to be broadcast across the airwaves.

While *facts* must be reported, some *facts* are conveniently sidestepped and it's no secret that the media has always had double standards. Hence the need for valid competitors that will hold the mainstream media accountable and propagate an unequivocally righteous standard.

Yet, who is willing to go? Who in this generation is saying, "Lord send me"? That's no longer referring to some distant far away mission field, but to the local, national and international media.

How the Mighty have Fallen!

Sure, the fight is real. It's intense. And yes they are bigger and stronger, just like Goliath was, yet still was no match for pure hearted David. In the same way, we are told above, "God will put them in your power," "conquer them... make no treaty with them." So, who will stand up and be counted? Who will allow God to position them, to conquer? Who is willing to slay today's Goliath - the media?

In this moment let's consider Millennials, specifically those who are on fire for God, and who possess unique capabilities when it comes to technology. We are told that they are tech-savvy, digitally native and organic! But this has been *gifted* to them, by virtue of the times that they live in and the generation they were born into. Still, gifts are not to be held. Joseph could interpret dreams. That gift made way for him, but it was for the greater good, to serve the bigger picture.

On the issue of ego and narcissism, put the spotlight back on Joseph. He couldn't have gone any higher up the ladder, save becoming Pharaoh himself! But that was never the intention. So who will stick with God's blueprint, regardless? Who will die to self, long enough, to carry the mission through? Can Millennials really carry this sort of responsibility? *Will...* they?

Giants do fall. And when they finally do, "Oh how the mighty have fallen!" Recently Hollywood mogul Harvey Weinstein has been toppled from his power post, for allegations of quid-pro-quo, harassment and sexually lewd misconduct stemming 3 decades. But in his prime, no one was willing to take him on. He was too powerful. Now, shamefaced Hollywood A-lister's are being questioned about their silent compliance and for looking the other way.

Exposing just how disingenuous feminism is in Hollywood being anti-Trump but *NOT* pro-women - as they claim. Their lecturing hypocrisy glares for all to see.

The only fear that the people of God should relent to is the fear of God, although the daily tsunami of bad news steadily eats away at our defences. It takes an unbending commitment to God's truth, to keep our eyes fixed on Him.

> ***Thou wilt keep him in perfect peace, whose mind is stayed on thee:*** *because he trusteth in thee. Trust ye in the Lord for ever: for in the Lord Jehovah is everlasting strength:* ***For he bringeth down them that dwell on high;*** *the lofty city, he layeth it low; he layeth it low, even to the ground; he bringeth it even to the dust...*

> *With my soul have I desired thee in the night; yea, with my spirit within me will I seek thee early: for* ***when thy judgments are in the earth, the inhabitants of the world will learn righteousness...***

> ***Lord, thou wilt ordain peace for us:*** *for thou also hast wrought all our works in us.*
>
> (Isaiah 26:3-5,9,12 KJVS)

Dr Alan

ENDNOTES:

1. "Media, Spiritual Gateway" by Drs Alan and Jennifer Pateman, Copyright © 2018, Published by APMI Publications

2. This "Truth for the Journey" has been taken from: https://watchersofthe4kings.com

3. Scripture references marked KJV are taken from the King James Version of the Bible.

4. Scripture references marked KJVS are taken from the Strong's Concordance with KJV. Taken from the TecartaBible App, © 2017 Tecarta, Inc. Version 7.11.5. Used by permission. All rights reserved.

5. Scripture quotations marked MSG are taken from The Message. Copyright © 1993, 1994, 1995, 1996, 2000, 2001, 2002. Used by permission of NavPress Publishing Group.

6. Scripture quotations marked TLB are taken from The Living Bible. Copyright © 1971 by Tyndale House Foundation. Used by permission of Tyndale House Publishers Inc., Carol Stream, Illinois 60188. All rights reserved.

7. Scripture quotations marked VOICE are taken from The Voice™. Copyright © 2008 by Ecclesia Bible Society. Used by permission. All rights reserved.

24❖

Spiritual Gateway – Media

Truth for the Journey
20th October 2017 – Watchers Letter

The Definition of Media

Hello again and welcome to this second part on the subject of media. **Hittites** were mentioned first in the line up of seven major gateways. I'm chiefly going to refer to *media* in the context of being a news outlet, simply because other angles of media will be addressed when we deal with *entertainment,* later on in this series *(see my book).*[1]

*Seven nations, all greater and mightier than you are: the **Hittites,** the Girgashites, the Amorites, the Canaanites, the Perizzites, the Hivites, the Jebusites. **When the Lord***

your God delivers them over to you to be destroyed,
do a complete job of it.

(Deuteronomy 7:1-2 TLB)

As we saw in part 1, the Hebrew definition of **Hittite** was all about FEAR. Mentioned first out of seven, for good reason, as no other spiritual gateway holds as much power as the media. Fear has great sway to influence everything that goes on in society; locally, nationally and internationally, including stock markets and the global economy.

However according to Revelations 21:7-8, we are destined to conquer not be defeated or beaten down by fear. In fact if we surrender our lives to the propaganda of fear, then God is not pleased at all.

So how do we define the media? The dictionary says that it's: "the main means of mass communication *(broadcasting, publishing, and the Internet)* regarded collectively." The platforms it uses are radio and TV stations, news networks and outlets, newspapers and magazines, Internet websites, opinion sites, blogs and much more.

News travels faster than the speed of light in today's world. It can circle the globe countless times before we can count on one hand! The Internet makes news not only travel faster but also greatly more accessible and widens the audience to even younger demographics, unparalleled to any other time in history.

Censorship, Monopoly and Groupthink

Part of media's power is its ability to censor information in order to control the narrative. Companies such as Facebook and Google for example, hold dangerous monopolies; even have as much revenue as some countries do! In fact Investopedia is quoted as saying, "Google's revenue beats the GDP of several major countries." Calling the company, "Google Nation" and its employees, "corporate citizens."

Media can incite public outrage over political issues while at the same time muffling stories that warrant massive exposure. Interviews can be deliberately *spliced* to misrepresent and mislead.

Fake outrage can be incited. Like the crowd that demanded Barabbas' release opposed to Jesus', *(perhaps the very same crowd who shouted **"Hosanna,"** not so long before!)* Media counts on the feckless and spineless principles of any *crowd*. Today, this can be referred to as *groupthink,* which according to the dictionary is, ***"the practice of thinking or making decisions as a group, resulting typically in unchallenged, poor-quality decision-making."***

Misinformation can be deliberately fed to the public so that by the time it's been officially *retracted* or *corrected,* the damage has long been done. Stories can be spiked or widely disseminated, depending on who is pulling the strings at the top. Partisan agendas, special interests, lobbying, bribery, elite conspiracy, cover-up and corruption, are all part of media's territory.

So it's safe to say that media, as a news outlet, is not a reliable source of impartial facts any longer, but a mechanism for *indoctrination.* Media has always flirted with danger because of its ability to shape public opinion. However, in today's environment and aggressive censorship practices, freedom of speech is either - public enemy No.1 or an elaborate myth.

Needless to say that media's reporting is not always accurate and though the use of propaganda is not new, it still has a new handle - *Fake-News!* Nothing exposes fake-news like politics, where elections are won and lost, based on the information that is fed to the public. The same public who take their generously cultivated *opinions* to the ballot box! Propaganda has been rebranded for today's savvier audience.

Left Leaning Media Pushes Socialism on Millennials

Conservative news and information services have been elevated in recent times, but they come under heavy fire from the left. Now more than ever, in this politically charged climate, *misrepresentation* is endemic. Take for instance socialism, which is trending specifically amongst Millennials, because they have no way of grasping the consequences of going down that particular path. They have no go-to experience, in their own lifetime, to get up close to.

Learning-by-experience is lost on them because they are experiencing much of this stuff for the first time around and aren't willing to listen to the menacing warnings of history. Naïvely supposing that their new and enlightened version of socialism can offer modern improvements on a failed system that has arguably *never* worked, anywhere in the world that it has been implemented, to date. *(Just ask any struggling Venezuelan who can't afford toilet paper, if they agree!)*

In fact, we are going to see more of a push towards socialism as time progresses, especially from the far left. And the more "Left" of the political spectrum that the media leans, the more favourable they are going to become. After all, Socialism is a control mechanism. It makes it easier to control people. While history teaches not everyone acquiesces, especially when they *realise* they're being exploited. The mainstream media that used to stand up against such things are more and more in the bag.

Tall and short of it is this: media is a major information gateway and in the wrong hands can create a dangerous monopoly. We have to offer an alternative.

We have a choice to make. Either we point out everything that's wrong with media or we turn the tables and control this unopposed force, for good. To build up media empires that use these vastly influential means to herald the truth of God.

Joseph – God's Catalyst who went Viral!

First let's consider what aided Joseph, to live in the times that he did and not be swayed by the culture. He was a man of God who became second only to Pharaoh. His position was a result of divine strategy, even though he lived in a deeply pagan society *(polytheistic and ritualistic not Judaeo-Christian)*. In other words his boss and counterparts didn't share his belief system!

What's your point? Joseph had to function deep inside an ancient Egyptian system, without it getting deep inside of him. He remained righteous and divinely positioned in order to help serve and save that society. *(Not to mention, preserve the lineage of Jesus Christ).*

So, Joseph was God's change-agent at a crucial juncture in history. He was the lynchpin and catalyst for systemic change, without being changed himself. This is our model. We are to go into the market place, where corruption dwells and allow God to raise us up. We need to understand God's positioning and bring His righteous influence from deep within and from the top down. Some of us are like modern Trojan horses, uniquely anointed and positioned to infiltrate the world's system from the inside out. *(Not window-shopping outside-looking-in).* We've got to get *inside* the culture in order to impact it - not vice-versa.

Bear in mind though, that Joseph's preparation for this position was intense. Why? He had to be able to handle it. His foundations had to run deep, so not to be toppled by the very culture he was injected into. Our God is a master strategist. He gets results, if we follow and obey His plan and not our own egos.

Pharaoh may not have changed much. Egyptian society might not have changed much, but God got His desired result. So not everyone out there in society is going to be saved, just because we show up, still God's strategy will play out, all the same.

Today God has no less ability to position you, his change-agents, who can go "viral" into the blood stream of society, culture and the media.

Stay blessed,
Dr Alan

ENDNOTES:

1. "Media, Spiritual Gateway" by Drs Alan and Jennifer Pateman, Copyright © 2018, Published by APMI Publications

2. This "Truth for the Journey" has been taken from: https://watchersofthe4kings.com

3. Scripture quotations marked TLB are taken from The Living Bible. Copyright © 1971 by Tyndale House Foundation. Used by permission of Tyndale House Publishers Inc., Carol Stream, Illinois 60188. All rights reserved.

25❖

A Geo-Political Drama Being Played out Across the NATIONS

Truth for the Journey
4th December 2020 - Watchers Letter

Remain Watching

Unmistakably this "end-time" period that we are in right now is all about NATIONS and KINGDOMS, as mentioned in the bible. Ezekiel 38-39 describes the Lord's great victory over the nations. The Gog-Magog war is mentioned, which is unfolding as we speak! *(See also Revelation 20:7-10)* When nations fight nations, it's a geopolitical war. Geopolitical refers to a combination of political factors: geography, economics, and demography, including foreign policy.

In geo-politics there are no real friends or enemies, only friendly enemies or hostile friends.

-- Unknown[1]

We see geo-political affairs played out on our screens every single day like a giant chess-board-drama involving powerful international players *(the nations of the world)*. Some like to say that politics is in a constant state of flux and massively *"unpredictable."* Whereas I'd rather propose the opposite, that politics is predictable based on the bible and how it guides us through history and teaches us about *"set times"* predicted by the Prophets, which must come to pass before Jesus returns.

This war is the beginning of a series of wars that will engulf the world in what many will call World War III. **The bible calls it Armageddon.** *You don't need to be a geopolitical expert to know that our world is coming apart at the seams. We are racing toward the end of the world as we know it.*

-- Pastor John Hagee

The Beast Rises out of The "SEA"

Daniel said, I saw in my vision by night, and behold, the four winds of the heavens [political and social agitations] were **stirring up the great sea [the nations of the world]. And four great beasts came up out of the sea in succession, and different from one another.**

(Daniel 7:2-3 AMPC)

Then I saw a wild beast rising from the sea *with ten horns and seven heads. On its horns were ten royal* *crowns, and on its heads were blasphemous names. It was like a leopard with feet like a bear's, and its mouth like the mouth of a lion. The dragon shared his power, throne, and great authority with the wild beast.*

(Revelations 13:1-2 TPT)

In both passages of scripture above, we see the Beast/s rising out of the sea *(the nations)*. AND the four kings mentioned in Daniel 7 are already taking up their positions as the bible predicts. During this epic power grab all four kings take centre stage – at once – and that time is now! We are in that *"set-time"* predicted well over 2,000 years ago and being fulfilled before our very eyes.

*A day of the Lord is coming, Jerusalem, when your possessions will be plundered and divided up within your very walls. **I will gather all the NATIONS to Jerusalem** to fight against it; the city will be captured, the houses ransacked, and the women raped. Half of the city will go into exile, but the rest of the people will not be taken from the city. **Then the Lord will go out and fight against those NATIONS, as he fights on a day of battle.***

1. The King of the East - China

China represents a military superpower that fears no other nation on earth. Described as the "East" or "sun rising" in the bible, we know this refers to China. This particular king is predicted to lead a mammoth army that will march in numbers exceeding 200 million soldiers, as described in scripture.

The king of the East is distinguished by his number, colour, and flag. The three frogs or three demonic spirits that seduce him will get them to come to the Battle of Armageddon. Armageddon is the mother of all wars. **It will be fought on the sacred soil of Israel for global supremacy between the King of the West and the King of the East. The pending prize is the throne of the earth, to rule and reign.**

-- *Pastor John Hagee*

2. The King of the North - Russia

Although the word "Russia" doesn't appear in the bible, its geographical position is located with exact precision. AND Putin who has slowly yet methodically been rebuilding the Russian Empire, believes he can master the world!

3. The King of the South - Egypt & Arab Islamic Forces

When Ezekiel speaks of Persia, Ethiopia, and Libya, he's speaking of the Arab Islamic nations. BUT, where God is concerned, always it is the city of Jerusalem that's the centre of the universe! This will be Christ's earthly home address. Really? Because when He returns, we know that His feet will "touch-down" on the Mount of Olives ("X" *marks the spot!*)

4. The King of the West is America and the UK

This king will be led by the antichrist, who will force every person to receive his mark on their right hand or forehead. Those who do not comply will be decapitated. The target of the King of the West is Israel. He will set up his image and proclaim that he is god in the city of Jerusalem. **The** *antichrist will demand that the world worship him. His false prophet will call fire down from heaven to consume the sacrifice laid upon the altar, emulating the Prophet Elijah on Mt. Carmel.*

-- Pastor John Hagee[2]

We know these kings are already in position and fiercely contending for the top spot. **YET they will face-off with non-other the King of kings and Lord of lords, who will rule and reign undefeated and supreme forever!**

He shall reign over the house of Jacob forever; and of his kingdom there shall be no end.

(Luke 1:33 KJV)

Of the increase of his government and peace there shall be no end, upon the throne of David, and upon his kingdom, to order it, and to establish it with judgment and with justice from henceforth even forever. The zeal of the Lord of hosts will perform this.

(Isaiah 9:7 KJV)

Let us remain watchers of these kingdoms. The antichrist and the false prophet are preparing themselves.

Yours in Christ,

Remember, We are Bigger than Religion, we reign with Christ Jesus, Amen.

Dr Alan

ENDNOTES:

1. https://www.urbandictionary.com/define.php?term=Geo-politics

2. https://www.jhm.org/Articles/2019-03-01-bible-prophecy-revealed. Excerpts used only in part and paraphrased

3. This "Truth for the Journey" has been taken from: https://watchersofthe4kings.com

4. Scripture references marked AMPC are taken from the Amplified® Bible (AMPC), Copyright © 1954, 1958, 1962, 1964, 1965, 1987 by The Lockman Foundation. Used by permission. www.Lockman.org

5. Scripture references marked KJV are taken from the King James Version of the Bible.

6. Scripture quotations marked TPT are from The Passion Translation®. Copyright © 2017, 2018 by Passion & Fire Ministries, Inc. Used by permission. All rights reserved. ThePassionTranslation.com

❖

Ministry Profile

Since its inception in 1987 Alan Pateman Ministries *(a Christian-based Para church, non-profit and non-denominational outreach)* has developed across the globe, but now is focusing on three main areas:

1. "Connecting for Excellence" (CFE) apostolic network, is a multi-facetted missions organisation with the purpose of connecting leaders for divine opportunities and building lasting relationships. Apostle Alan has to date ordained more than 500 ministers in over 50 nations. In addition there are ministries, churches and schools who are in Association or Affiliation, looking to him to provide spiritual oversight, personal mentorship and accountability.

Yearly conferences are being hosted *(where possible)* in different locations, to provide support and encouragement.

2. Secondly, the teaching arm "LifeStyle International Christian University" (LICU), founded in 2007, is a study program for students who desire to invest time from their lives into university studies where they can receive from the Anointing of the Word of God; not only to receive academic credits but an impartation that brings personal transformation. The same program can be applied for correspondence studies including identical syllabuses and study material designed for distance learning. Resulting in the same certification at the end of their studies! Degrees offered at our university range from a "Diploma in Theology" to a "Doctor of Philosophy" for those who decide to go through the full university program.

LICU is a global network of universities, operating from different nations *(overseeing correspondence students and regional campuses)*, with a board of executive directors, professors, national directors, faculty members and administrational staff. These national directors and teams work with the International Head Office, located in Italy. Our purpose is to demonstrate the Supernatural Kingdom of God through Doctrinal, Apostolic and Prophetic Teaching.

Graduation ceremonies are held every year in different nations, such as Cameroon, the Netherlands, Italy and so on.

3. Media - known as an accomplished author and prolific writer, Dr Alan has published over eighty books *(to date)* and teaching materials, *(that have been made available in most formats).* For example, his popular online **"Letters to the Church"** called, Truth for the Journey, has developed a worldwide audience, including the newest venture, **Watchers of the 4 kings.**

To summarise, Dr Alan is Founder and President, CEO of **Alan Pateman Ministries International** (APMI), with his international Head Office located in Italy *(overseeing national offices in different locations),* and which umbrellas the following apostolic ministries:

- Connecting for Excellence Apostolic Network – Founder/ Overseer
- LifeStyle International Christian University - Dr Alan holds the position of President, CEO, Professor of Theology,

Biblical Studies and Apostolic Ministry *(currently LICU is exploding throughout Europe, Asia and Africa)*
- International Apostolic Accreditation Council
- APMI Publishing and Publications / Media

On a personal note, Alan the family man, who grew up on an English farm, still enjoys long walks in the countryside with his family today. Still an avid walker, he spends many hours in the Tuscan hills and beautiful coastlines! Beyond his primary passions *(family and Christ)*, Alan has a very creative eye and innovative flare. As a talented artist, Alan loves painting large modern abstract canvases, but all forms of art and design are always stimulating to him, especially architecture and interior design. Not excluding the fact that Alan has always designed his own media materials, book covers and websites etc.

However, no matter how busy life gets, Dr Alan and his wife Jenny appreciate being surrounded by family and friends, children and growing number of grandchildren. They reside in Lucca, Tuscany *(The Eagle's Nest)*, Italy.

Alan Pateman Ph.D., D.Min., D.D., M.A., B.Th.

ENDNOTES:

1. The Eagle's Nest is a prophetic vision that God gave to Alan in 1996. He said, "Italy is your Nest *(Ministry International Head-Office)* and from it you will fly out, to and fro, to the nations."

2. Dr. Alan Pateman attended several colleges throughout his training *(including studying Theology at Roffey Place, Horsham, UK and a Member of Kerygma - with Rev. Colin Urquhart and Dr. Bob Gordon - 1985-1987)* before being awarded a Doctorate of Divinity *(2006)* in recognition of his lifetime achievements by the International College of Excellence, now "DanEl Christian College" *(President: Dr. Robb Thompson USA)* also "Life Christian University" *(Dr. Douglas Wingate USA)* where he also earned a Bachelor of Theology B.Th. *(2006)*, a Master of Arts in Theology M.A., a Doctor of Ministry in Theology D.Min., *(2007)* and Doctor of Philosophy in Theology Ph.D. *(2013)* from LICU.

❖

To Contact the Author

Please email:

Alan Pateman Ministries International

Email: apostledr@alanpateman.com
Web: www.AlanPatemanMinistries.com

*Please include your prayer requests
and comments when you write.*

❖

Other Books

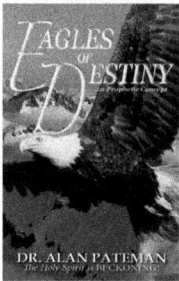

Eagles of Destiny ...a Prophetic Concept

In this book, we can learn the secret of RESTING in the Lord and not wearing ourselves out living by pseudo and nervous energy that gets depleted quickly and can't be replenished. God alone is our source and supply.

ISBN: 978-1-909132-20-7, Pages: 16, Format: Paperback, Published: 2022 *Also available in eBook format!*

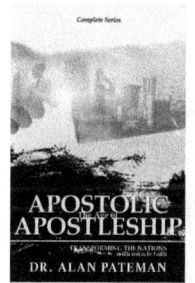

The Age of Apostolic Apostleship (*complete series*)

In order to view how the Apostolic baton was successfully passed from one generation to the next. Knowing that through the perseverance and obedience of others - history as we know it was altered forever. Dr Alan Pateman, a modern day apostle (ascension) looks to reflect on their testimony in this wonderful book.

ISBN: 978-1-909132-65-8, Pages: 420, Format: Paperback, Published: 2017 *Also available in eBook format!*

Truth for the Journey Books

Israel, the Church and the End Times
(End Times - Complete Series)

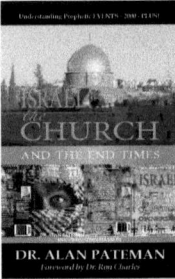

Within the pages of this book (which has to be a "must-read" for any serious enquirer into the Healing and Deliverance Ministry), Dr Alan unfolds a different pathway, so that the heartbeat of God's message of God's total deliverance can be released into the church of Jesus Christ today.

ISBN: 978-1-909132-77-1, PAGES: 448, Format: Paperback, Published: 2018
Also available in eBook format!

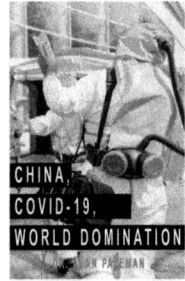

China, Covid-19, World Domination

Church, this period is a wake up call. The world uses the term "woke" to describe this. The church must be "woke," but not to the propaganda and deception of this world, but to the truth of what God wants to do in the earth today.

ISBN: 978-1-909132-85-6, Pages: 132, Format: Paperback, Published: 2020
Also available in eBook format!

Media, Spiritual Gateway

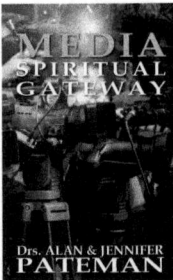

Let's face it; we live in the era of fake news! It's always existed, but never been quite so prominent. Today it's an all-out-war between fact and political fiction. The media has been sabotaged by political activism. Gone are the days of impartiality and objective unbiased reporting, with many sources saying that true journalism is dead.

ISBN: 978-1-909132-54-2, Pages: 192, Format: Paperback, Published: 2018
Also available in eBook format!

Dear Friends,

Have you considered becoming one of our international students? We are privileged to welcome you, from around the world, to "LifeStyle International Christian University" *(the teaching arm of Alan Pateman Ministries International).* **An English speaking university** dedicated to your success; to see you trained and equipped to fully succeed in your God given Destiny.

It is our passion to raise up the leaders of tomorrow, who will have influence in all realms of authority, including the Body of Christ. Men and women of strategy, wisdom and true godliness, who'll stand with stature and maturity in this hour.

It's undeniable that in today's world, recognised education has become indispensable, therefore it is our desire to offer well balanced and well structured courses. Those that have been written by gifted and talented ministers of God, who seek to be inspired by God's Holy Spirit.

Consequently we have put together a **flexible curriculum,** designed both for correspondence students and campuses, which is a strategy to reach the distant learner; whether provincial, national or international. In fact we have many correspondence students from around the world, including a growing number of successful campuses, in various countries.

This is a growing platform, where men and women of dignity and passion, can grow and be established in their God given endeavours. As God is the healer of the nations, we pray and believe that many of our alumni will go on to **become world changers** in their own right.

We are proud of each and every one of our LICU students.
It would be our pleasure if you would join them on this incredible journey!

Doctor Alan Pateman

Alan Pateman Prof. Ph.D., D.Min., D.D., M.A., B.Th.
PRESIDENT AND CEO
www.licuuniversity.com www.cfeapostolicnetwork.com
Email: info@licuuniversity.com   Mob: +39 366 329 1315

For more information visit our website/facebook or contact our office, using the details below:

Website: www.licuuniversity.com
Facebook: www.facebook.com/LICUMainCampus
Email: info@licuuniversity.com
Telephone: +39 366 329 1315

www.ingramcontent.com/pod-product-compliance
Lightning Source LLC
Chambersburg PA
CBHW071525040426
42452CB00008B/884